Distributed Leadership and Digital Innovation

"Longstanding views that favor heroism in leadership are coming to an end. This book is an excellent contribution to our understanding of alternatives to the way leadership is exercised in twenty-first-century organizations. The book is refreshing and opens up really important debates, especially in a time in which alternative ways of organizing are emerging."
—*Dr. Jose Bento Da Silva, Warwick Business School*

"Maniscalco makes a compelling case for Couple Leadership, the new paradigm for leadership within the digital sector. By dissecting the model and analyzing its practice, she lays bare the benefits it brings and how it navigates the pitfalls all too often succumbed to in traditional approaches to the role of digital innovation. Engaging from an academic perspective, her hypotheses are backed up with real-world explorations and practical tools to put the theory into immediate use in the workplace, making this a must-read for digital innovation leaders, both old and new, as well as those working in proximity to such business functions."
—*Prask Sutton, CEO of Wi5*

When it comes to digital innovation, much research has been done with regard to the optimization of teams, but little attention has been given to leadership structures. This book presents a comprehensive research background on innovation leadership and its evolution over the years, examining how it has been shown to reflect the thinking needed today for organizations to succeed.

This timely book proposes a refreshing and contemporary perspective on leadership that aims to address many of the challenges that leaders in digital innovation are faced with every day. With insights and experiences from other digital innovation leaders, as well as an auto-ethnographical case study, it will be of value to researchers, academics, practitioners, and students with an interest in leadership, innovation management, digital innovation, organization studies, and organizational psychology.

Caterina Maniscalco is a partner at a management consultancy firm based in London. She has 20 years of global experience across a wide array of industries in the fields of digital innovation and digital transformation. Informed by a multidisciplinary background that includes technical development, design disciplines, coaching, and strategy, her areas of focus in recent years have been leadership excellence, culture and behavior change, and experience design.

Routledge Focus on Business and Management

The fields of business and management have grown exponentially as areas of research and education. This growth presents challenges for readers trying to keep up with the latest important insights. Routledge Focus on Business and Management presents small books on big topics and how they intersect with the world of business research.

Individually, each title in the series provides coverage of a key academic topic, whilst collectively, the series forms a comprehensive collection across the business disciplines.

Ephemeral Retailing
Pop-up Stores in a Postmodern Consumption Era
Ghalia Boustani

Effective Workforce Development
A Concise Guide for HR and Line Managers
Antonios Panagiotakopoulos

Employment Relations and Ethnic Minority Enterprise
An Ethnography of Chinese Restaurants in the UK
Xisi Li

Women, Work and Migration
Nursing in Australia
Diane van den Broek and Dimitria Groutsis

Distributed Leadership and Digital Innovation
The Argument For Couple Leadership
Caterina Maniscalco

For more information about this series, please visit: www.routledge.com/
Routledge-Focus-on-Business-and-Management/book-series/FBM

Distributed Leadership and Digital Innovation

The Argument For Couple Leadership

Caterina Maniscalco

Routledge
Taylor & Francis Group

NEW YORK AND LONDON

First published 2020
by Routledge
52 Vanderbilt Avenue, New York, NY 10017

and by Routledge
2 Park Square, Milton Park, Abingdon, Oxon, OX14 4RN

Routledge is an imprint of the Taylor & Francis Group, an informa business

© 2020 Taylor & Francis

Library of Congress Cataloging-in-Publication Data
Names: Maniscalco, Caterina, author.
Title: Distributed leadership and digital innovation : the argument for
    couple leadership / Caterina Maniscalco, MBA.
Description: New York, NY : Routledge, 2020. | Series: Routledge
    focus on business and management | Includes bibliographical
    references and index.
Identifiers: LCCN 2019044444 | ISBN 9780367361488 (hardback) |
    ISBN 9780367363659 (ebook)
Subjects: LCSH: Leadership. | Technological innovations—Management. |
    Information technology—Management.
Classification: LCC HD57.7 .M35554 2020 | DDC 658.4/092—dc23
LC record available at https://lccn.loc.gov/2019044444

ISBN: 978-0-367-36148-8 (hbk)
ISBN: 978-0-367-36365-9 (ebk)

Typeset in Times New Roman
by Apex CoVantage, LLC

Contents

3 The Couple Leadership Model 35

Conclusion 48

Preface

In the spring of 2015, I was approaching my wits' end. I was working 80-hour weeks, providing digital consultancy and delivery services to a very important although challenging global client, while completing my MBA at Warwick Business School. My colleague and boss in this endeavor had a combination of personality characteristics and project expectations that at times made him difficult to manage, and I had also decided to take four modules that semester so I could graduate six months early. It was a stressful time during which I was very uninspired.

It was at this time that I attended the well-known course taught by Hari Tsoukas called "Leadership and the Art of Judgement." This was easily the most inspirational course of my MBA and—very possibly—my life. It forever changed my perception of good leadership, increased my awareness of my own actions and behavior, empowered me to better manage workplace crises and challenges, and developed my understanding of what drives individuals who work with or for me to bring the best of themselves every day. Anyone in a leadership position—corporate, political, familial, or otherwise—should be required to take this course, and repeat it annually as a refresher; in fact, if Britain's political leaders had taken this course, we could have probably avoided the Brexit ordeal (but I digress).

Prior to Tsoukas' course, I had intended to complete a dissertation on digital marketing—but by the third day of the module, I felt invigorated: I knew I had to begin again and change my focus to leadership studies. I applied the lessons from the course to the digital career experience I had acquired over the years, and applied both to the leadership challenges I experienced in my past and present roles. The final result was a dissertation entitled "Managing Risks, Failure and Challenges in Digital Innovation: The Argument for Couple Leadership," which was awarded a distinction mark.

In recent years and with my experience of digital innovation and transformation programs in Europe, Asia, and North America, I found remarkable how many of these continued to face the same challenges—nearly all of them stemming from the leadership level. All too often, organizations attempt to address their innovation challenges by solely focusing on the staff doing the "doing"—as if creating Agile team structures and sending teams on a design thinking workshop without critically examining their own leadership can magically resolve all their challenges. It's more than understandable why this is the case; many of the themes in this volume explore this. However, without a similar examination of leadership—structurally, culturally, and otherwise—long-term digital innovation success will continue to be a painful endeavor.

In the development of the work you are presently reading, I restructured the research and insights from my dissertation for an improved flow and ease of reading. Whereas the dissertation was purely academic, here I have reduced or removed more tedious content related to research methodology and added real-world examples of personal, professional experiences to bring the material to life. I have also provided references to additional topics for greater context, particularly a section on culture, and updated the bibliography accordingly.

If you are a digital innovation leader, business owner, management consultant, digital agency professional, or in any way involved in this highly dynamic industry, there is something in this volume for you. I hope this work will help ease the discomfort that inevitably comes with digital innovation leadership, raise the potential pitfalls before they become issues, and support the development of positive and empowering organizational cultures that motivate, fulfill, and drive staff and leadership alike.

Introduction

Context

Andrew Carnegie once said, "No man will make a great leader who wants to do it all himself, or to get all the credit for doing it" (Kruse, 2012).

Nearly 20 years' experience in a variety of industries and sectors (including digital marketing and advertising agencies, management consultancy, nonprofit, and in-house client roles) has given me a front row seat to the exciting journey that has been the evolution of the digital arena. Today, the sheer quantity and variety of professional roles in this space varies tremendously: digital strategists, user experience specialists, user interface design, mobile app developers, web developers, front-end and back-end developers, creative technologists, testers, social media managers, and so much more. However, it is heartening to remember that, prior to the 1990s, when the expansion of the World Wide Web was in its early days, many of these roles didn't yet exist. Web professionals in this space were often responsible for every stage of the process, including user and stakeholder consultation, interface design, web development, testing, and everything in between (Compton-Hall, 2014; Casserly, 2002; Smart Insights, 2015).

Today, entering the digital space is no longer an option but a necessity to sustain any competitive advantage, and innovation is accepted a necessity for growth and survival. This need has led to the development of new roles such as Chief Innovation Officers and Digital innovation Directors. Similar to the nascent state of the Web in the late 1990s, digital innovation professionals today have responsibilities spanning a wide array of disciplines—often with expectations and demands that go far beyond what may be appropriate for a single individual.

Professionals in this field face a constantly changing environment with continuous uncertainty, risk, and inevitable failure as part of their role. This in itself creates concerns regarding the manner in which leader performance in this sphere can and should be appraised. The demands of such a position don't attract the cautious or the risk averse; rather, roles like these are particularly attractive to those with heroic and narcissistic leadership personas. Consequently, they are also subject to the pitfalls that often accompany these personas (Maccoby, 2002).

Purpose

This volume proposes replacing the default leadership model—that of the solo leader we are accustomed to—with that of the couple leadership model in which two people share the role, particularly in digital innovation. It explores the current challenges with the present model, and presents the unrealistic expectations placed on innovation leaders as well as the current leadership model's vulnerability to the downfalls that come with heroic and narcissistic leadership.

I aim to demonstrate the benefits of the couple leadership model and how it (1) compensates for the downsides of the narcissist leader, (2) avoids the hero leader paradigm, (3) reduces risk of failure, (4) establishes healthier working cultures and conditions, (5) promotes diversity of thought, (5) sets an example of collaborative working for teams, and (6) distributes the responsibilities and uniquely high pressures of the innovation professional. It is an innovative leadership model for an innovative role: one that has already been proven successful in other industries, is particularly suited to this application, and is indeed already emerging in the field of digital innovation.

Scope

The scope of the primary research that underpins this volume was originally focused on leadership models in small to medium businesses rather than large corporations. These are organizations such as startups, or digital agencies whose clients may include such large corporations. They are businesses that operate on tighter timescales and require greater agility than the large corporations who turn to them to support their innovation plans. These small and medium businesses prioritize creating change, customer focus, and organizational learning for these flexible and externally focused firms. Many of them do not have innovation steering committees or innovation governance committees, but due to business size or purely convention, they have a Digital Innovation Director or a Chief Innovation Officer responsible for digital innovation leadership. However, the principles underpinning the model are relevant regardless of size. Therefore, it should be possible to extend the same leadership model to larger corporations as long as the distributed leadership model is applied, and innovation teams within these businesses are given an adequate degree of autonomy to function as their own unique entities so that they may retain the necessary degree of agility.

Before we continue, it is important to clarify some of the nomenclature used throughout this book. For our purposes, the definition for digital innovation is "the creation and successful delivery of new digital products and services" (Kahan, 2013, p. 159). The definition of "leaders" that I prefer is

> those do or cause to be done all that must be done and is now not being done to achieve what we say is important. They provide a sense of purpose, direction and focus. They build alignment and get commitment.
>
> (Deschamps, 2008, p. 7)

I'm particularly fond of this definition because it avoids references to hierarchy. Time and time again I've seen inspirational leadership from individuals who don't hold top leadership positions. This is especially relevant in innovation projects, as they typically thrive best in flatter structures.

As you move on to Chapter 1 in this volume, you'll be exposed to research, concepts, and issues that relate to innovation leadership. Chapter 1 provides a foundation for contextualizing the material that follows in Chapter 2, which explores these topics through the real-life experiences and perspectives of innovation leaders. By this stage you should have a thorough understanding of the challenges in digital innovation leadership and sufficiently appreciate how the couple leadership model can alleviate these challenges. Chapter 3 explores this model, presents a case study demonstrating this model at work, and provides recommendations for implementing the model in your own organization. A brief summary conclusion follows, with recommendations for the couple leadership model and benefits of its application in the field of digital innovation. Supporting anecdotes from my own career are dispersed throughout as well.

Please note that although I outline the challenges of innovation leaders and discuss the techniques, approaches, and methods that are common to this field, I do not provide a detailed exploration. There are many books already available on topics like Agile methodology, fail-fast approaches to iterative development, design thinking, and more. They are disciplines worthy of their own volumes and are enablers to digital innovation that should be explored in their own right by anyone operating in this field. But, they are beyond the scope of the present volume.

Data and Research

This research was conducted in a fast-paced period of the digital era when digital technology and innovation has moved beyond the domain of graduate students in Silicon Valley to mainstream corporations and international service firms. Although most organizations have now accepted the notion that they need to embrace innovation to remain relevant, many are still apprehensive. This hesitation often stems from a lack of subject matter expertise, or from the inherent risk in any kind of innovation when one does something for the first time. Regardless of the cause, however, hesitation can lead to slower growth and loss of competitive advantage, and loss of relevance and heightened stress for the business in such a position (Kaplan, 2012).

The data on which this book is founded includes three sources. The first is firsthand experience from nearly 20 years in the field, including an auto-ethnographical case study for more in-depth insight.

The second source consists of a collection of six in-depth, anonymous, semi-structured interviews that were digitally recorded, a summary of which can be found in Chapter 2 in this volume. I specifically selected male and female individuals in the United States and the United Kingdom who held the roles of Digital Innovation Director, Innovation Director, and Chief Innovation Officer and worked for agencies or accelerators. Private businesses turn to these firms for their expertise in innovation, which is regarded to require specific subject matter specialty, highly skilled resources, and the experience to manage the risks incurred.

After the completion of interviews, the more traditional secondary literary research was conducted in order to allow for a more focused research process. The results of this third data source are presented according to the overriding and recurrent themes that presented themselves (Ellis, 2004; Ellis et al., 2011).

1 Innovation Leadership Landscape

Although digital innovation leadership is a growing field in recent years, it was surprising to discover what limited material is available on this topic at the time of research. Although there is ample research available in relation to leadership and innovation—including leadership of creative teams— there was limited research material available that specifically and directly relates to *digital* innovation leadership, especially if focusing on small and medium businesses.

But general innovation leadership material does provide a good starting point for exploring our most relevant topics, and sheds some light on how resolving this complex challenge has been approached thus far. For our purposes, I've shaped the conversation around three key themes: innovation leadership as a topic in and of itself, risk and failure (arguably the biggest challenge in innovation), and the leader persona, with emphasis on narcissistic leadership in innovation.

The Elusive Formula for Innovation Leadership Success

In 1989, researchers Westley and Mintzberg explored different styles of "visionary" leadership—the kind of leadership that is capable of driving important, meaningful change and innovation. They examined personas, or role types, such as the idealist, the diviner, or the bricoleur, among others. In some ways, this might recall the early days of digital careers when professionals found themselves providing the services of designers, developers, testers, and more—all in one person. And so, like 20 years ago, the challenge here is that the innovation leader is expected to be a combination of *all* the personas.

This is a rather tall order, and arguably an excessive request from a sole individual. The digital landscape is more complex; there are far more channels to consider; there is a better understanding of the myriad of personas and their wants and needs that need catering for in a personalized manner;

the world today is far more digitally saturated so that the impact of a digital professional today has the potential for far more reach. The risks for an innovation leader today far outweigh the risks of the solo digital professional from two years ago.

More recently, Seth Kahan's (2013) research on what is required for successful leadership in innovation clearly portrays the complexity of the role. Good ideas aren't sufficient for success. Kahan cites seven activities a leader must master, which he describes as the ability to identify market shifts with regard to one's organization's position, build internal innovation capacities, collect intelligence, shift one's perspective (we might call this open-mindedness), exploit disruption, generate value, and drive innovation uptake. Kahan (2013) himself recognizes the immense task that is asked of an innovation leader, and acknowledges the phenomenon of "innovation stress" that leaders are required to manage (and do so to varying degrees of success). In a moment in time when, thankfully, awareness of the importance and impact of mental health and well-being in the workplace is increasing among employers, there is all the more reason to confront this challenge in a constructive manner (CIPD, 2019; Wilson, 2018).

Kahan's (2013) perspective is that some of this innovation stress is productive, and this is understandable to a degree; I imagine a great many of us have experienced moments where we "thrive under pressure" and experience some of our most productive moments under stress (this volume is no exception). At times when it becomes too much pressure for the individual, Kahan advises addressing this with greater structure—but he falls short of questioning if the answer truly is to add more of the structure that creates these circumstances to start with, or to opt for a new, different framework that better supports innovation.

The innovation stress that accumulates is even more burdensome in light of the expectation that it is either not supposed to be there or it is not supposed to be noticeable; the innovation leader always appears cool, calm, and confident. Part of the role, as we explore further shortly, is the instilling of confidence in others to the degree that they feel more comfortable with the inherent risks involved, and thereby easing the anxiety the rest of the organization is experiencing in their transformation. However, the relationship between self-confidence and creativity—a key ingredient for innovation—has been demonstrated by researchers (Mumford and Connelly, 1991), and supports the conclusion that innovation leaders must feel assurance in having permission to fail in order to be successful, regardless of the innate stress of the role.

But the risk is noteworthy. In the words of Sternberg (2003, P. 397), "Creativity does not happen in the absence of risk taking." According to Mumford et al. (2002), this risk comes from three risk sources: there is no guarantee that an idea will be viable, no guarantee that it can be developed, and no guarantee it will be successful—both in implementation and in the market. There are approaches and tactics that can be used to limit and mitigate these risks, but experimentation and failure tolerance—as well as the tensions that will inevitably arise as a consequence—must be embraced by organizations.

Interestingly, the researchers also noted that the "emergence of multi-functional teams may have placed a new premium on breadth—as well as a depth—of expertise in the leadership of creative ventures" (Mumford et al., 2002, P. 737). We are seeing this come to the fore in most recent years, as generalists are waking to a new appreciation for their breadth of background (Epstein, 2019). This demand for a broader understanding of multiple disciplines simultaneously creates a greater degree of risk (argu-ably, more wide-ranging accountability may lead to more opportunities to make poorer choices) and puts heightened pressure on one individual to take on greater responsibility.

With the acknowledgment of the range of skills required, Mumford et al. (2002) did consider a new approach that consists of a three-part model, separated into idea generation, idea structuring, and idea promotion. But the persistent question remains: How can any one person effectively pursue these three distinct types of activities at the same time? By this point it is hopefully becoming clearer that the requirements expected of an innovation leader are possibly too extensive for a solo individual.

Deschamps and Nelson's (2014) publication on innovation governance aimed to address many of the pressures that Kahan (2013) and others raise, and did so through a robust framework that includes a strong focus on a designated body: an Innovation Governance Committee. The committee is assigned responsibilities that they collectively take ownership for, includ-ing the promotion of entrepreneurship, collaboration and curiosity, as well as the management of the business risk profile and failure tolerance. Des-champs and Nelson (2014) also considered leadership styles and defined six attributes they feel are essential to the innovation leader: a combined bal-ance of emotion and realism, acceptance of risk and failure, the wisdom to understand when to end projects, the ability to attract innovators to build and steer teams, an openness to external approaches and ideas, and a contagious passion for learning and innovation.

Rather than a skill set, the preceding attributes describe a highly specific persona and mind-set, which we'll explore further in the coming sections. The main challenges I would put forth to the approach of Deschamps and Nelson (2014) presented here, however, are three: (1) like most material available on the subject, the authors discuss innovation in broad terms rather than specifically digital innovation (which brings with it additional chal-lenges and layers of complexity); (2) they place heavy reliance on innovation governance committees, which may be present in large corporations but not in the small to medium businesses; and (3) the bureaucracy and additional governance that comes with a committee or similar body inevitably stifles the pace of innovation. In some cases, I've seen the addition of a committee or forum to an innovation operational framework add months to a project and years to a wider program (one such case is described in the case study in Chapter 3; another example was that of a global bank whose innovation committee was scheduled to meet once per month, and more often than not decision makers did not arrive—thereby delaying project funding and sign-off for months).

All three of the preceding challenges are reasons for which traditional corporations ultimately turn to agencies for digital innovation projects that embrace much of the risk involved. This governance committee approach formalizes innovation leadership in a way that is not agile enough for those businesses aiming to be pioneers in the fast-paced digital arena, and consequently contrasts with digitally innovative cultures. In one of Deschamps' case studies, a business is even lauded for maintaining the same steering committee for over a decade, something that in my experience would be unheard of, if not frowned upon, in the digital agency sector.

It can be argued that corporate governance teams can also be myopic, and often governed by corporates rather than subject matter specialists with technical or digital experience. Also, the larger they are, the more they risk groupthink—and pose an inherent risk as a consequence (Conforth and Brown, 2014).

I witnessed cases of these latter points personally in my career on several occasions. I recall a particular occasion some years ago in which, as part of a wider global digital transformation program, I was responsible for presenting new digital solutions for reducing the duration of call center conversations in which consumers purchased financial products. Customers were kept on the phone for absurd lengths of time due to the legal obligation the business had to present them with terms and conditions prior to purchase completion. The solution involved the presentation of terms and conditions content in a digital and secure manner that was both efficient and cost-effective. The business could either choose an off-the-shelf solution from a third-party provider that met some of the requirements but would incur indefinite subscription costs and an (at the time) unclear understanding over data ownership, or they could opt for a custom technical solution I designed for them that met all of their requirements, was more secure, more cost-efficient, and would clearly ensure that all data and intellectual property resided with the business. As you may have guessed, the business chose the third-party solution, and I later learned there were important relationships among the corporates and the third-party that insisted it would be this way; any counterargument in the early debates was suppressed. Furthermore, in the presentation I prepared for the committee that would ultimately decide the solution, I was asked to submit my presentation to be checked and approved in advance, to ensure that the content would be presented in such a way that would favor the third-party solution.

The preceding case is not only a great example of how risk can sometimes be exasperated by corporate governance committees; but it demonstrates how poor innovation choices can be made that hold an innovation leader as an owner and potential scapegoat although his or her (and even their team's) expertise has not been treated as valid. This sets a bad scene for organizational culture, and for team motivation and drive. I am particularly fond of Daniel Pink's (2011) view of what drives professionals in this modern world: autonomy, mastery, and purpose. When a leader is shackled by a large committee (loss of autonomy), and when their expertise is not given due credit (loss of mastery), it's only natural for one to ask "what's the point?" (loss of purpose). Issues will inevitably develop as a result.

Defining Innovation Leadership Success

With all these challenges and demands on our innovation leaders, how does one go about determining fairly if they are succeeding in their roles? With regard to their performance assessment, there is little material presently available. The publication by Innovaro (2008), "Innovation Leaders," attempts to address the topic to some degree, but provides an assessment of leading innovative businesses rather than individuals within the organization. Still, the criteria they use for assessment sheds some light on the topic. Among these criteria are organizational culture and support structure; strategic focus on innovation and its role in driving corporate growth; number of major new product launches and relative success ratios; growth in revenues, profits, and market capitalization; average revenue and margin per product or customer; investment in innovation-related activities (i.e. R&D, marketing); brand value and human capital growth; peer review from within the sector; and, where appropriate, intellectual property performance.

Two points are noteworthy observations here. The first is the strong correlation that is assumed between a successful leader and a successful innovation—regardless of the uncertainty, risk, and factors out of the innovation leader's control that may influence an innovation's success. In fact, most businesses performance appraisals and reward systems do not question this (Deschamps, 2008), and it is of paramount importance that it is addressed because it has profound implications on the establishment of a healthy innovation culture, which we will explore further. The second is the peer review, which puts weight on the value of reputation—a factor that will be a consideration in the decision-making process of an innovation leader. It feels necessary to ask if these criteria should be factors in such evaluation at all, and, if so, to which extent is appropriate—but this is out of scope and could (perhaps, should) be the subject of another volume entirely.

It seems logical that a sound basis for performance evaluation first requires a shared understanding between organization and individual on the expectation of the role and on what it means to be a leader. As a reminder, Deschamps (2008) defines leaders as those who

> do or cause to be done all that must be done and is now not being done to achieve what we say is important. These individuals provide a sense of purpose, direction and focus; they build alignment and get commitment.

Based on this definition, leadership is a process in which the end result is less important and the assessment criteria should reflect this accordingly. On this basis, he recommends a shift from a financial focus, and prefers one based on the stimulation of innovation drivers, culture, and values as well as the effectiveness of the innovation process rather than the innovation itself. The practicality of the matter needs consideration, however, and I have yet to come across an organization that would not put direct or indirect financial targets on an innovation leader and the performance of his or her team.

The literature on innovation leadership consists of a varied array of opinions regarding the requirements for success in this field, and all of it puts forth a daunting view. Researchers Makri and Scandura (2010) suggest the leader be both focused on both the external and internal environments, while promoting the acquisition of new skills as well as commercializing them. They introduce two dimensions of strategic leadership: operational leadership, which is focused externally and is concentrated on opportunities for knowledge development, and creative leadership, which is focused on creating an organizational culture that embraces curiosity and risk (a topic we will explore further in the next chapter). Although both dimensions are important, they choose to prioritize creative leadership for innovation growth. Although they provide two interesting dimensions through which to view innovation leadership, I would argue they fall short by positioning their argument as if the option were only one or the other. But, as it is unlikely to find an individual that can drive both strategic leadership styles simultaneously, we find again the need for a new leadership model that can adequately address this.

In 2008, Deschamps' research on innovation leaders also put a spotlight on the unique challenges of this emergent role. He presents four leadership styles: the warrior, mentor, judge, and diplomat. In an implicit understanding that all four styles in combination with all six of his aforementioned essential attributes are challenging to find in one individual, he broke leaders down into two types: front-end innovation leaders (focused on ideas, concepts, and technology) and back-end innovation leaders (more operationally focused). He also considers a combination of a "Mr. (or Ms.) Creativity" and "Mr. (or Ms.) Discipline," among whom the ideation and operational responsibilities are divided. It's a convenient arrangement for the innovation leaders who Deschamps describes as—inconveniently—more interested in being creatively focused, rather than owning the financial responsibilities that form part of innovation leadership. Naturally, the ideal for any organization would be a combination of all these, as it is essential that the financial responsibilities are, in fact, acknowledged and assumed. It is in this area that arguably the greatest challenge for a digital innovation leader is found: management of the risk and potential failure (financial and otherwise) of the proposed innovation.

Risk and Failure in Innovation Leadership

> Every situation that works has been built on a mistake. When engaging with a complex world, failure is inevitable. Failure in our assumptions, our theories, our methods and our strategies. The hallmark of great institutions, now and throughout history, has been a capacity to leverage these failures in the dynamic process of change. Institutions founded on authority, on defensiveness, on a lack of courage to engage with mistakes, have held the world back in many ways.
>
> (Syed, 2015, p. 93)

It is widely accepted that innovation—digital or otherwise—requires the acceptance of failure for progress, but the threshold of acceptance of failure varies greatly among organizations. In the matter of leader appraisals in innovation (particularly the digital kind), the success or failure of an innovation appears to be a significant factor. The risk tolerance of a business influences the degree to which an innovation leader will be granted a "license to fail," something essential for a leader's effectiveness in a field of such uncertainty and inevitable failure (based on the sheer impossibility of every innovation developing into a successful one). There are of course many approaches that innovation leaders and organizations use to minimize this risk—be it validation through stress-testing ideas by welcoming dissent and critique, creative exploration of ideas and their resonance to different audiences through design thinking practices, and the "fail fast" philosophy that has become so intrinsic in iterative development and Agile methodology. But the role, and the innovation (product or otherwise), can never be entirely risk-free, and when projects fail, the innovation leader typically takes the blame (Giessner et al., 2009; Scott, 2017).

Performance appraisals impact the perception—positive or negative—of an innovation leader and his or her ability to influence. Research by Kollee et al. (2013) demonstrates the direct impact of such evaluations on teams and followers, and even states that the appraisal result can often be driven by external factors such as even the mood of the appraiser on that day. Appraisers are human, after all (for now, at least), and they have bad days—and this is only considering appraisers that operate with conscious integrity. The world is full of stories of professionals penalized for reasons that are less than above board, and over time I have witnessed countless occasions of unconscious bias and conflicts of interest. It would be naïve at best to believe it doesn't exist. But the research also raises the concern that these assessment outcomes—sometimes based on flimsy foundations—have a noteworthy impact on future performance by the leader when risk-taking is a central part of the role. The fundamental message here is that the more an organization embraces risk, the less a failure is deemed to be a bad thing, and the less that factors like mood will have an influence, hence affecting leader evaluation less poorly. This, therefore, allows the leader to be more comfortable taking risks, consequently increasing organizational performance (Kollee et al., 2013).

With innovation ideation, Mumford and Licuanan (2004) also cite timing as another influential factor in the appraisal of ideas generated. They acknowledge that performance of idea generation and idea implementation shouldn't be appraised the same way, arguing that routine or normative efforts should not necessarily be viewed through the same lens as creative efforts. Their research focused on circumstances in which a leader is responsible for a team who is tasked with idea generation, but in cases in which the leader is responsible for—or a participant of—the idea generation process (as would be seen in smaller, more agile, digital environments), the lines become blurred and the task is more complex.

It stands to reason that while it may create metaphorically blurry, messy lines, the teams in which ideation is a collaborative exercise are also those which minimize risk. In teams that have succeeded in creating a sufficient degree of psychological safety, there will be opportunities for conflicting opinions to be raised—sometimes even in a formalized way. Many of Silicon Valley's most renowned companies, such as Apple and Google, create space and time in their processes to welcome debate and dissent to better inform and more fully understand the strengths and weaknesses of an idea (Scott, 2017).

To add further complexity to the issue of idea appraisal, Mumford and Licuanan (2004) highlight that a leader's motivations behind innovation choices are shaped by perceived environmental opportunities and risks; but surely this would include not only the organization's exposure to such risks and opportunities but also those of the leader as well—both within the organization and in terms of his or her reputation in the industry. Research by Hall et al. (2004) argues that perceived leader performance "redefines or reinforces leader reputation . . . (and) leader style." So, the risk of a diminished reputation is an influential factor in the innovation decision-making process, which may serve as a kind of accountability, but will also deter a risk-averse leader. And, the conspicuousness of the role and its high-profile nature is likely to also deter the careful and "quiet" leader Badaracco (2002) speaks of as well.

The Narcissistic Leader Persona

Alas, careful and quiet leaders are hardly common in this professional space. With uncertainty, appraiser moods, timing, risk, and chance among key factors that innovation leaders must navigate for success, it is not surprising that roles like this appeal to those who will not be led by fear but by their own confidence: typically the hero and narcissistic personas. Of the three types of leader personas outlined by Maccoby (2002) (the others are the erotic/nurturing persona that is typical of teachers and caregivers, and the obsessive/efficiency-centric persona that is typical of those in operational roles), those with a dominant narcissistic side are natural characters for this position.

Narcissism comes in both constructive as well as reactive or destructive variations, and need not always be negative. It is believed that leaders need some level of narcissism to drive confidence and tenacity, as well as creativity. The passion, risk-taking, and boldness required to push businesses to new heights can be relied on these "maverick" individuals, as Deschamps (2008) calls them (Coutu, 2004). Constructive, or productive, narcissists tend to be strategically creative and embrace risk-taking that drives the digital transformations many understand to be necessary. They not only take the chances called for, but through charisma and charm, they can grow followers that support them (Coutu, 2004; Maccoby, 2002).

But this quality in these typically charismatic leaders can have negative consequences as well, and the followers who tend to idealize them may place themselves in a vulnerable position as a consequence. This idealization has been closely linked to the Freudian concept of transference in which individuals see in their leader the powerful figures of their formative past (often a teacher or parental figure)—and stressful periods as well as hierarchical circumstances often trigger this (Coutu, 2004). As risk and uncertainty is so innate to innovation, and the short timescales of the digital arena only exacerbate this, it would seem reasonable to follow that the leader in this situation who accepts this stress is thereby viewed (albeit unconsciously) this way to some level. And when the idealization is present, it is also reasonable to expect the leader's risk decisions to be less questioned and doubted as a consequence. Stein's case study reflects this, arguing however that instead of there being constructive narcissist leaders and reactive narcissist leaders, all leaders possess the ability for both—and that stress, such as that from an economic downturn in Stein's case, would cause any leader to become a reactive narcissist. This is inherently problematic in a field like innovation in which uncertainty is the daily norm (Coutu, 2004; Maccoby, 2002; Stein, 2013).

Maccoby (2002) makes recommendations for the management of a narcissist in an organization, some of which are not easy to implement. For example, encouraging a leader to pursue analysis or psychotherapy may not be a warmly received or embraced recommendation—although Campbell et al. (2009) make a strong argument that all leaders should undertake this anyway, as they are all subject to unconscious bias and self-interests, as well as distorted attachments and memories that are the root of many poor decisions. However, he also recommends providing the individual with a "sidekick," someone the leader can trust and develop a close relationship with, someone who will keep the leader grounded. Ideally, this individual would be of a particular temperament, with a heightened sensitivity to understand how best to manage the relationship, thereby requiring a level of emotional intelligence somewhat higher than what is already demanded of leaders. The fictional examples of narcissist Don Quixote and his sensible Sancho Panza serve to describe the dynamic well. But more interestingly, with this recommendation, Maccoby (2002) indirectly makes the recommendation for distributed leadership in these cases (Campbell et al., 2009; Goleman, 2004; Maccoby, 2002).

2 Digital Innovation Leadership

Firsthand Accounts

Candid Accounts

Imagine for a moment that your organization has asked you to lead a team in the design, preparation, and presentation of a five-course meal for an awards night. Your task is to present a dining experience that is inspiring, new, and unlike anything served in previous years. Attendees are VIP caliber; it's a career-defining opportunity.

You've been assigned a team composed of the world's best chefs in their disciplines, be it patisserie, fish, meat, and everything in between, who have never worked in a kitchen together before. You don't have a clear number of attendees, their dining preferences, allergies, or other considerations. Your brief is simple: You must present something new and different that delights attendees and puts your organization in glowing light; if you fail, it will reflect poorly on you and likely cost you your position. After all, the team all reports to you: You make all the important decisions.

If you can imagine this experience—the uncertainty, the unrealistic demands and expectations, the egos involved, and the appetite for risk this undertaking involves—then you can imagine a day in the life of a digital innovation leader.

* * *

Thus far, we have explored innovation leadership to understand its multifaceted challenges from a predominantly theoretical perspective. By this point, you, the reader, are beginning to see that there is good reason to consider alternative leadership models beyond that of the solo leader. Hopefully it will be an even more compelling argument when you explore in this chapter how these leadership challenges manifest in reality through the accounts of those who experience life in the role on a daily basis. By the end of this chapter it is hoped you will begin to see how the default leadership model is not suited to digital innovation, and how this sector is a particularly appropriate and advantageous one in which to introduce the couple leadership model.

For your reference, Table 2.1 provides a summary of the six digital innovation professionals who were interviewed (names have been changed for anonymity), and Table 2.2 provides a full summary of the interview insights collected from the interviewees.

Table 2.1 High-Level Interview Profiles

Alex	Innovation Director at an advertising agency; London-based
Brian	Director of Innovation at an experiential agency; London-based
Chris	Global Digital Director of Innovation at an advertising agency; New York-based
Dana	Digital Innovation Director at a multichannel accelerator; London-based
Eric	Chief Innovation Officer at an agency and startup; London-based
Felix	Director of Innovation at an in-house agency; London-based

Table 2.2 Interview Data From Digital Innovation Leaders: Key Highlights

Previous roles, experience	Alex	Creative Director
	Brian	Account Management, Creative, Planner, Strategist
	Chris	Planner, Mathematics, Strategy, Tech & Ecommerce, Business Director, Accounts Service
	Dana	Sales, Ops, Marketing & COO
	Eric	Physics, Philosophy, Computer Science, Copywriter, Music Business, Experiential Events, Multi-sensory
	Felix	Web Developer, Project Manager, Client Managing Director, Strategy, Head of Digital, Head of Digital Strategy
Leadership qualities leaders felt are needed in the role	Alex	Inspirational, able to develop and execute a vision; contagious positivity and excitement
	Brian	Patience, restlessness, resilience, confidence, great collaboration skills
	Chris	Strong team management skills, encouragement of authenticity in teams
	Dana	Forward thinking, user focus, curiosity, can-do attitude, risk awareness, ethics, understanding connections between products and human behavior
	Eric	Patience, appreciation of work from various disciplines, able to allow some autonomy
	Felix	Willingness to assume responsibility for success and failure; understanding which battles to pick

Perceived requirements for success in role	Alex	Wide curiosity about the digital world, ability to extrapolate usefulness from digital
	Brian	Experience, awareness that there is no one-size-fits-all approach, ability to form partnerships, very senior support, influence, forgiving yourself
	Chris	Strategic thinking, understanding changing business landscape, info on a wide range of fields
	Eric	Understanding tech and adoption drivers, membership/influence among industry, wisdom in digital tech application
	Felix	Leadership (create and execute a vision), ability to rally people to vision, digital expertise, clear roles for team, comfortable to fail and embrace risk, thick skin, legitimacy within the business, ability to deal with non-followers
What they bring to the role	Alex	Takes lateral leaps to make connections, storytelling, sales skills
	Dana	Experience with cross-country and cross-cultural teams, can navigate stakeholders and opportunities
	Eric	Encourages passion and proactive, collaborative behavior in teams, encourages risk-taking and making mistakes
	Felix	Breadth of expertise, happy to take responsibility for possible failure, can "roll with the punches," being a "specialist generalist"
Organization's success measures	Alex	Selling and delivering quality work
	Brian	Various KPIs, revenue, generating profile for the agency, social ROI
	Chris	Real-world (over traditional agency) measures
	Dana	Commercial value, growth of companies in innovation startup network
	Eric	Client and staff happiness, nature of work being done, pride among team
	Felix	Team/360 feedback, impact to business, client feedback, recognition from broader sector or industry
How they measure success	Alex	Influence
	Chris	Client trust, ability to establish frameworks
	Dana	If industry considers her a point of reference for trends; establishment of partnership events, attendance at events
	Eric	Whether he loves coming to work
	Felix	How much he loves what he has done

(*Continued*)

Table 2.2 (Continued)

Their position in the organization	Alex	Influencing, inspiring, involvement in execution
	Brian	Within leadership team; close to Financial Director
	Chris	Within accounts team; works with strategists
	Dana	Management team; co-founder
	Eric	Small, flat team structure—is a co-founder
	Felix	Within leadership team; inspires innovation adoption, assembles disparate teams, facilitates rather than directs
How they foster innovation	Alex	Labs: the R&D unit of the agency; SXW1 (agency-sponsored event); agency culture of doing things differently
	Brian	Dedicated innovation space; speaking at industry events; internal sharing sessions 2x per month
	Chris	Nothing done: people are either interesting, creative and vibrant—or they're not
	Dana	Pioneer stakeholder is always present in meetings to sell innovation through their influence
	Eric	Lead by example; give people nearly impossible tasks (encouraging breakthrough thinking)
	Felix	From top down: company must be designed around innovation; ensure people appreciate what you're doing; engender vision among lieutenants who carry it forward; small steps and trial cases
Key challenges	Alex	Clients don't think of them first for innovation work; role fights to be seen as a must-have rather than luxury
	Brian	Digital consultancies such as Accenture or IBM moving in as key competitors; relationships with different clients that have more budget
	Dana	Desire for startup-type growth among very traditional businesses
How teams work	Alex	Agile and collaborative approach; connects disciplines
	Brian	Proximity builds affinity: disciplines sit near each other; empathy: judicious on challenges; takes collaborative over disruptive approach
	Chris	Encourages authenticity in teams
	Dana	Previous experience with team hired specifically for optimal efficiency
	Eric	Encourages contribution; promotes the wearing of multiple hats; collaboration; avoids pulling rank; encourages people to work on own ideas then share with wider team
	Felix	Builds teams—rarely inherits them; finds five or six lieutenants who know how to work with him to avoid managing too many people; encourage collaboration through shared areas, avoiding big amorphous groups, developer involvement from start

Who makes the final call?	Alex	Creative director
	Brian	Managing partner team
	Dana	Three co-founders collectively
	Eric	If hard decisions are required, senior management; otherwise, collaborative
	Felix	I do, based on experience, intuition, and gut reaction
Conflict or disagreement management	Chris	Very limited
	Dana	Conflict usually around project prioritization; evaluation of long-term vs. short-term goals
	Felix	Is it a problem that affects project quality? Is it someone "kicking off"? How passionate is individual? Do I trust their passion and experience? Will the idea get bought? I make the final decision: there's only one person deciding
Managing hesitant clients	Alex	Ease them in
	Brian	Clients concerned about budget and repercussions: address solutions with this in mind; invest only if risk can be afforded; projects more than three to six months is too long
	Chris	Give clients a vision and also a concrete map of how to get there
	Dana	Sell vision to pioneer first, he can sell to other stakeholders
	Eric	Innovation means risk for clients, but people want a world-first: role requires management of fears and expectations, giving them tools to understand; build trust so they know you won't do anything to put them in jeopardy
On partnership/ co-leadership	Alex	With creative director
	Brian	With Finance Director; compares to Steve Jobs/Tim Cook relationship; yin/yang of financial vs. opportunity cost
	Chris	No partnership
	Dana	One of the other co-founders; have healthy debates
	Eric	Business partner. Encourages debate, breeds honesty, forces thinking before action, gives emotional support, stops people from becoming megalomaniacs
	Felix	Looks for (junior) lieutenant to use for management/ manipulation of situations; "At the end of the day, I take the risks and get the rewards"; power is always with the money, which is controlled by client, who looks for most senior person

(*Continued*)

Table 2.2 (Continued)

Investment decision factors	Brian	Scalability, synergy, personnel involved, hard cost to business vs. opportunity cost in terms of research
	Dana	Long-term vs. short-term priorities
	Felix	Is benefit worth time and investment cost? Good talking point for the client? First mover advantage? Will tech be successful? How can it be used? Good PR?
A selection of final thoughts on innovation:	Brian	It's fundamental to see the human behavior and experience to inform innovation.
	Chris	Innovative should be the description of the solution, not the solution itself.
	Dana	A big problem is the corporate world needs to become more agile. Can be done by building cluster teams, part in-house, with different experts; anyone can build an innovation space; real challenge is changing people's mind-sets.
	Eric	You should always be onto the next thing. You should be 18 months ahead of what you're showing to clients.
	Felix	Innovation that is packaged up and resold stops being innovation. Be willing to take risks; be a good gambler. Take informed risks and be willing to take responsibility for successes and failures.

Business Decisions and Prioritization Criteria

Internally, the obstacles to success that digital innovation leaders are facing within their organizations today go beyond the typical concerns of skills shortages in the team or tight deadlines. In some businesses, their role is still fighting to be seen as a must-have rather than a luxury in meetings; the relevance and impact of this position is still being questioned. Alex has experienced this firsthand, and in my professional experience I have often seen meetings organized by senior roles such as the Global Head of Innovation rescheduled and pushed back regularly, as if innovation is the lowest priority matter that a business needs to address.

However, when their role within the business is validated, the challenges are many and varied—and where to invest their limited resources is one of the biggest challenges. For example, Dana finds herself regularly in the position of prioritizing between the long-term versus short-term priorities of the business, which can feel like a constant tug of war.

Other factors also enter the decision-making process. For Brian, scalability, the actual hard cost to the business in comparison to the opportunity cost of research, and even the synergy among participating stakeholders as well as the actual personnel involved are all considered before deciding to pursue an opportunity. Synergy and professional chemistry are so significant to a successful project that his business has in the past turned down work based on which particularly difficult stakeholders from the client's side would have been involved.

Felix also considers if the benefit is worth the investment of time and effort, but factors in strategic value as well: "Is this innovation a good talking point for the client? Is this piece of technology going to be successful and generate good PR? How will this be used once in the market?" If the project will lead to a first mover advantage, then the project becomes all the more desirable for him.

External challenges are present as well. Competition for digital innovation work has been increasing, especially so with established digital consultancies like Accenture, IBM and others now moving into the areas of design thinking, service design, and experience design, which have previously been owned by agencies and smaller boutique businesses. Budget holders are changing too: Chris finds that agencies have thus far had close relationships with marketing teams in businesses, but their budgets have been shrinking, whereas Chief Technology Officer budgets have been growing (and Chief Data Officers in particular, in recent years), so new relationships are required to pursue meaningful business growth.

Managing Risk

Innovation implies new, unchartered territory and no guarantees of success; the risks involved make clients nervous and apprehensive. To further complicate this challenge, the perception of these risks is sometimes highly subjective, depending on everything from personalities, values, and culture, and largely affected by unconscious biases such as affect heuristics. Digital innovation leaders face these matters on a daily basis, and with their own different approaches (Kahneman, 2012).

When addressing risk with clients, Felix, Dana, and Alex believe in starting small to ease in clients gradually with the discomfort they feel in operating in this new world. As Alex describes it to his peers, "The first murder is always the hardest." Over time, one builds a trusted relationship, making it easier to take the next chance, and the one after that.

Trust is fundamental in human relationships in general, but all the more so when risk is involved. I recall a project in which I was responsible for the strategy, design, and development of a new digital experience across what would be eventually over 20 markets. The client operated in a heavily regulated industry and was naturally risk averse as a result. Part of the experience design included a social media element that wasn't just a gimmick, but directly supported the underlying strategy. As you can probably expect, this was strongly vetoed by the Risk Lead. After days and nights of lengthy conversations, we eventually came to a compromise on how we would incorporate social media in a way that would limit the risk to the brand to a degree she felt comfortable supporting. We both operated from the perspective that we wanted the best possible experience for the end customer, and having a shared mission was an important starting place. All that was needed after that was a trusted relationship in which she felt that I would not put her career or her company at risk to achieve this. To achieve this aim, emotional intelligence and a personal code of integrity and respect will take you farther than any accolades or extensive digital experience.

However, it usually takes more than one person to come onboard with a large strategic piece of work. And, because trust is so essential, Dana drives the message that building a relationship with an influential pioneer within the business is a strategic key to driving necessary change in the wider business (to help persuade others to support new ideas), but each client is catered to differently:

> Tier-one companies are nervous because their ways of operating the business are quite traditional. . . . You also need to take into account a lot of stakeholders, you need to have the pioneers within the company, those will help push it over the border. . . . The more flat the organization is, the easier it is. . . .

Brian find that his clients invest only when it is a risk they feel they can afford, as they are concerned with two primary issues: how much will the project cost, and will it get them fired. He designs solutions with this in mind:

> [For clients:] one, it's about money, and two, it's will this get me fired . . . when talking about clients and innovation is, in terms of churn rate from jobs, it's typically two to three years. So that gives you a very finite window to get an innovation away. If you're talking anything beyond three-to-six months you're talking about a time period which is too long. . . . I think if you make it accessible from a "will it scale quickly" and it's money that I can afford to risk—because some innovation is a kind of gamble.

Sometimes the issue is based in expectations: Chris finds that clients are often stuck between where they are and what they know now, and the often far-fetched, unrealistic pictures of the future that many agencies pitch. He prides himself on developing a vision for them of where they want to be, as well as the concrete steps that will get them there. Eric has found that often, clients want a "world-first," which is problematic because he feels if it has not been done before, it is because it hasn't been thought of; it cannot be done; or it should not be done, for reasons that may not be immediately clear—and this is partly where risk is rooted. In this case he views management of fears and expectations to be his key responsibility in this role. For those who are more hesitant, like the other interviewees he, too, slowly builds up trust over time until the client feels comfortable that they would not take any action that would put their job or client in jeopardy.

But Eric feels the entire point of being innovative is that the individual *should* always be onto the next thing: If something is being shown to the client, this person should already be 18 months ahead of whatever innovation they are demonstrating. And, by being more transparent with clients to the point of making them comfortable with the innovation, they are more likely to trust the advice they are given and invest further.

In contrast, Felix believes that sometimes it is less important to be first and more important to do it best—thereby progressing a more rudimentary piece of innovation on the market (it's a respectable argument; for example, while most of the world is familiar with iPods, I expect there are few who recall the first mp3 player, or the German company that invented it). Felix advises finding new ways of telling stories, keeping abreast of industry developments, and remembering that innovation can take on many forms. His point of insistence was, however, on the importance of being willing to take a risk; taking informed risks and taking responsibility for successes and failures is the best way to lead in innovation.

Risk can be reduced, according to Brian, by embracing a philosophy that the innovation should be a solution to a business problem so that the developed result is well informed. He finds that 90 percent of his projects develop this way, rather than developing a new innovation and then looking for an application for it. This is likely to be best practice for most businesses. However, Eric—whose business is partly that of an invention engine—does not feel he requires this. He feels they work in such a way that the market either needs what they have developed, or they know they can develop the need for it. In other words, they create both the demand and the supply to it. In my personal experience, the latter is by far the riskier pursuit, but it can create the greater reward by establishing pioneer products that, at least in the short run, have no direct competition.

Demands and Expectations

As we explored in the preceding chapter, the ambitious requests and expectations placed on leaders in digital innovation are many: being both internally as well as externally focused; creatively minded yet strategically oriented;

having a profound understanding of market movements; accepting risk; driving business growth through innovation successes; and instilling passion, collaboration, and a learning culture in teams among other requisites. Other skills for success include "big picture" strategic thinking.

When we asked Alex about the skills he feels are needed, he felt it essential to have a wide-ranging curiosity in the digital world as well as the ability to extrapolate usefulness from digital, thereby seeing applications that may not be obvious. This correlates with the need for breadth of experience that is required to make the less obvious connections that can drive innovation. As such, all individuals interviewed have a diverse, multidisciplinary professional background that consists of different yet complementary roles, including creative, technical development, strategy, client service, copywriting, and more. This supports previously presented findings from academics such as Mumford et al. (2002), indicating the emerging need for a wide breadth of expertise across multiple functions—a challenging requirement for a sole individual. This is also why, although Westley and Mintzberg (1989) identified different personas for visionary leadership, it is believed that this role requires a combination rather than one sole persona.

Interviewed individuals have also directly expressed the importance of understanding the work that different disciplines across the spectrum conduct in order to perform the team leadership function well. This is important for two reasons: first, it supports the adaptive, administrative, and enabling elements that are important in the leadership of complex projects. In other words, it allows a leader to understand the nuances of how each jigsaw puzzle in his organization can come together to make a whole picture: understanding the impact of a design change to the technical solution, or understanding how the change to the strategy affects a program's scope, timings, and budget. The second reason is rooted in the importance of credibility (Uhl-Bien et al., 2007).

This is why hands-on coding was an important requirement for Eric. He believes it's beneficial to "know what you're talking about when you're managing a team of people who do something." Felix responded similarly, as legitimacy within the business is essential for him, and he believes this comes from having strong knowledge rather than merely being "a good talker." Felix has an expression for individuals like himself; he calls one with his breadth of expertise "a specialist generalist."

In my own years of managing multidisciplinary teams, I have directly experienced the value that comes with having been a specialist myself, across multiple disciplines. For example, the nature of the conversations I have had with designers becomes more complex and engaging when they learn of my own design background, and my recommendations were always given greater consideration once my past experience was clear to them.

This was even more the case among the development teams I led. In what is still a heavily male-dominated sector, my credibility was rarely assumed. On one occasion from many years ago, after strange behavior among some in the technical team in the business I'd just joined, the technical director I was hired to replace took me through his own evaluative questions to assess my suitability to the role because he and the others assumed that the hiring manager "just met a pretty lady in the pub and gave her a job." Without my hand-on experience and ability to speak to the finer technical details, I would not have earned the respect of my team or worked as effectively as I did with them in my role.

However, interdisciplinary background is not only important internally; it also earns credibility with the client. As Chris expressed, ". . . it's hard to get respect from the client [without it]. You become a functionary about bringing (other) people into a room rather than actually contributing to the conversation and leading it." I, too, have experienced this firsthand; my career and client relationships have frequently benefitted from having the knowledge to speak about the details and constraints of a technical solution without depending on a member of the development team, while also understanding business implications and requirements to effectively inform a strategy or program.

None of the individuals I interviewed has an MBA or has had formal business training at the degree level. The lack of formal business preparation not only reflects Deschamps' (2008) findings that creative-focused innovation leaders may be less interested in the financial responsibilities of the role, it also indicates they may not be adequately prepared or comfortable with such responsibilities. This inevitably carries an additional element of risk to the role, which many of these leaders mitigate by collaborating with a partner such as a co-founder, or a Financial Director—as Brian explicitly stated he does. It is in this manner that his informal couple leadership relationship has developed.

A License to Fail

All individuals had views on the leadership qualities that were required for their roles, including development and execution of a vision, contagious enthusiasm, and collaboration skills. It was the importance of managing risk and accepting failure, however, that came to the surface repeatedly. Brian feels it is essential to also have confidence, self-assuredness, and resilience to deal with the setbacks that will inevitably appear. He says,

> . . . you can have 9 failures for every 1 success, so I think you have to be very patient. . . . You also have to be quite restless as well, so you

need to maintain a lot of energy to cope with the inevitable setbacks you get. . . .

In fact, some leaders work to encourage a fail-fast, risk-taking culture. When asked what they individually bring to the role, Eric felt his biggest contribution to the role was what he brought to the team: He cited encouraging his staff to take risks and make mistakes, as well as encouraging them to keep abreast of what's happening and to stay curious, sticking "their nose where (they might feel) it's not wanted." When embracing a risk-taking culture, Brian also cited the ability to be forgiving. Not all the chances one takes will be successful, and it is essential for Brian that individuals in the role can accept this—as well as the organization they work for:

> I think . . . in an innovation role . . . you need to be quite forgiving . . . if you don't hit 5 out 5 that fine. Obviously that's a feeling that needs to be shared by your boss as well. But as long as I've done as much as I can do in terms of employing different strategies I know work from experience . . . innovation by its very nature, you're trying to do things that are new, and therefore like any toddler they can trip and fall over. . . . I hate the cliché "permission to fail" but you do give yourself that, whether or not others do.

Research from Giessner et al. (2009) and Kollee et al. (2013) raised the importance of having a "license to fail," and the care an organization must take in associating a "failure" with that of a poor leader. Hirak et al. (2012) and Edmonson (1999) has also demonstrated the importance of psychological safety and its direct impact on performance. So, the organization's own innovation culture and associated tolerance for risk and failure must be high enough to allow for some failure if it is to grow. Felix expresses this, and how imperative it is to be comfortable to take a chance and fail:

> One needs to be comfortable to fail, because with innovation you're trying to sell stuff that may not have been done before, so . . . one has to be happy with the idea that certain projects will "fail" against objectives. As long as that failure can then be used as something to move forward. . . .

However, it is unclear how this manifests itself in a context in which performance appraisals are directly tied, at least in part, to innovation success and subsequent commercial metrics. All interviewed individuals made reference to growth or profit results as a key performance indicator in their organizations, so making the right decision is important. At least in the case of Brian, who works closely with his Financial Director in an informal couple leadership model, the risk is somewhat mitigated.

So what becomes apparent is that the pressure to succeed comes from two sources: partly from the organization and partly from the individual. From the organization's perspective, this can sometimes be exasperated by innovation successes having a delayed result—which becomes then a future investment and a risk in and of itself. Brian explained,

> Sometimes it's . . . finding the solution; not necessarily about the money that you make from applying that solution. Not necessarily in year one. Sometimes we have business plan KPIs where year one might be find a successful solution to this, year two is build it, scale it; year three is monetize it.

What is clear is that both the organization and the leader must be comfortable with risk-taking if they are to succeed in digital innovation. As Felix expressed,

> The biggest thing is about being willing to take a risk . . . you have to be almost a good gambler . . . the best gamblers don't make a bet unless they're pretty confident. . . . Take informed risks . . . and be willing to be responsible for the success and the "failure." That's probably the best way of being in innovation.

As if the uncertainty of a positive result following an innovation development and launch were not sufficient, the preceding requirements feed into the "innovation stress" phenomenon referred to by Kahan (2013) earlier. Surely leaders that have excessive responsibilities and unrealistic expectations on their shoulders would only create a situation of a heightened risk and increased potential failure in addition to that which is already inherent in the role. But what if this role simply was not designed for one individual alone?

In the early days of the internet boom as website development was emerging as a field, the web professional wore multiple hats, which, in today's more developed environment would have been split into career specialisms—including those of the front-end developer and the back-end developer who share the coding responsibilities. One responsible for the code that creates the appearance of the interface and the other for the database integration and complex functionality, these two roles are now understood to have unique skill sets and experience that are both required for the build of a professional website. As the emerging need for innovation leadership becomes more accepted, prominent, and understood among organizations, it is expected that this role will be understood to require very distinct specialisms that should not be expected of one individual.

This is especially so in light of the extent of the risk some leaders feel they are taking. Felix states that in his view, the extent of comfort with failure must be such that one is willing to "put one's reputation on the line":

> . . . being happy to take responsibility for what might be considered failure is something I've never shied away from . . . if someone says "well what's the proof?" The proof may just have to be "I think it will work. I'll put my reputation on the line and say we should do this." One has to know what one is talking about enough to be able to say, "I think this is a good bet."

This further confirms research by Hall et al. (2004), which provided the earlier conclusion that the risk of a diminished reputation among industry peers is an influential factor which deters those more risk averse.

Being comfortable with one's own abilities and confident in one's breadth of expertise to support a project that has no certainty it will succeed—to the extent that one would risk their professional reputation—is a very challenging role requirement to fill. However, in light of research from Mumford and Connelly (1991) that demonstrates the direct correlation between creativity and self-confidence, it is an essential one. It is for this reason that narcissistic personas have much to offer to this role.

Narcissism and the Leader Persona

There is no innovation without risk taking; without it, the result is the perpetuation of what Eric describes as a culture in which other people's work is merely replicated and re-skinned to appear different—which is not truly innovation. However, eventually risk aversion will bring organizational decline if it is not overcome (Kulas et al., 2013)—and narcissistic personas are naturally gifted in overcoming this aversion (Maccoby, 2002).

Fortunately, it has already been demonstrated that narcissism has a place in digital innovation leadership and can bring with it many positive results—especially as the relationship between creativity and self-assuredness is already in evidence. In fact, some level of personal glory must be sought in the evaluation of risky decisions when the evaluation of the individual in such a high profile role will grow or damage their reputation (Innovaro, 2008; Mumford and Connelly, 1991; Mumford and Licuanan, 2004).

One individual in particular, Felix, most clearly demonstrated the tendency of narcissism and heightened self-confidence in digital innovation leadership:

> Being happy to take responsibility for what might be considered failure is something I've never shied away from. . . . I know how to sell stuff to clients and engage them to want to buy. . . . I know how to come up with ideas, how to visualize the thing; how to create experiences; I know how it will be built, and I have a good idea how long it will take . . . my batting average is pretty good, I tend to come up with things that do tend to work. . . . I think that there aren't many people like that. . . .

Those positive narcissistic qualities such as vision, charisma, and the ease of developing a following are also instrumental to rallying support, convincing people who feel "it can't work" to become believers and supporters. It's an important trait for this leadership position—as Felix explains,

> you almost have to be a salesman for innovation as well. You have to be able to rally support. And you have to be able to deal with people that don't support you. The ideal for that would be to try to get them on side, but the worst case is try to mitigate their lack of support.

Regardless, as Dana cites, innovation will require taking chances, and self-belief is required: ". . . you have to be like a horse with blinders. . . . You get a lot of people telling you 'that can't work' and you just have to believe in it to make it work." As Maccoby (2002) indicates, however, this drive must be measured to an extent, and the narcissist leader will interpret a differing opinion as a challenge and threat. The recommendation to pair this individual with a partner that validates their thinking can offset the risk when there is one, and can offset the reaction to dissention when there is a need for it.

However, Felix would probably not warm to distributed leadership—and if so, only from a hierarchical perspective in which he had a subordinate. He believes "at the end of the day, I take the risks and get the rewards. . . . It's 'The Felix Show.'" Felix argues this position by stipulating that power always lies where the money is, which is controlled by the client, and the client will always ask for the most senior person—which he believes can only be one person.

He may not be wrong: it has already been established that the implicit and widely accepted view of leadership is comprised of a solo leader, but this does not mean it is correct or must be perpetual. Perhaps a truly innovative organization will live its values even through its innovative leadership structure, becoming a pioneer for a new way forward in leadership thought.

But for the moment, it is evident that Felix would benefit from a partner to keep him grounded, as cited by Maccoby (2004).

Culture

We have already touched on some key ideas around innovation mind-set that, by this point, will have suggested that establishing the right culture and behaviors within a team and organization is a predominant factor for success. Collaboration, psychological safety, and embracing challenges are important and recurring themes among the most successful innovative teams. Unfortunately, as Dana warns, while anyone can build an innovation space in their business, changing people and business mind-set and culture to embrace innovation is a real challenge without an easy fix. Dana finds that there may be a desire for startup growth in clients who have businesses that are typically very traditional. The corporate world needs to become more agile, approach team structures differently, and embrace different skills and experience—and this takes time.

Collaboration

There is plenty of literature and research that makes reference to the profound importance of collaboration among and across teams for innovation success (Deschamps, 2008; Deschamps and Nelson, 2014; Giessner et al., 2009; Hirak et al., 2012;). Every leader has his or her own approach to implementing this: Brian embraces a collaborative over a disruptive approach, and stresses the value in sitting teams near each other so that "proximity builds affinity"; he believes this also encourages empathy by allowing for increased understanding of what is happening and thereby increases judiciousness over which challenges are taken. Like Brian, Felix encourages teams to work well together by having commonly shared areas, but he does not believe in big amorphous groups because then people don't understand where their place is within the organization. He has also found that projects have been more successful when developers were involved in team meetings from the beginning.

Eric stresses the importance of hiring staff who are proactive contributors to ideas—even willing to take chances and express ideas in teams which are not necessarily their own. For Eric, this allows teams to feel greater pride in their work, which ultimately fuels collaboration further—like a self-propelling engine.

He recruits people that come up with great ideas that will embrace the opportunity to contribute, wear multiple hats and take chances:

> There was a philosopher called Carl Popper who was a big proponent of . . . falsification theory . . . you really learn something when you run

an experiment and you prove that something is false. . . . So we try to encourage that kind of ideology, that it's ok to get it wrong and screw it up, as long as you are screwing up for the same reason of, "never again" and not making the same mistake twice. Making a mistake is fine.

Senior managers are there only for course correction and they rarely pull rank, because they feel it engenders animosity. "If someone is going to work 48 hours straight to deliver a project, they will only do it if they believe in it Brian (an alias)." Autonomous working occasionally happens when people will work on an idea on their own to get it to a point where they can share it with a wider team in a way that can be more widely understood. This approach further establishes a healthy organizational culture in which the leadership traits among the whole team are nurtured and fostered (Uhl-Bien et al., 2007).

Brian raised the importance of considering external collaborative working as well when he cited the ability to form partnerships (with startups, incubators, and related parties in the industry), influence others, and develop very senior support from within the business. Eric also indicated collaboration as a key skill, believing it is key for fostering links in the industry:

You have to have . . . the ability to foster links with the communities that make these things and develop these things. Even better, become part of that community yourself so you aren't separated out from academia and research; you've got a foot in both camps.

I acknowledge that it is widely accepted that collaboration is essential to success. However, collaboration in an organization culture is not easy to embed: As Dana expresses, while anyone can build an innovation space in their business, changing people and business culture is still a big challenge.

One such example from my professional life came when I designed a framework that not only enabled new innovations to be developed and released faster but also was underpinned by processes and rites that enabled deeper and much-needed cultural change. Understanding the challenges that might be faced in this global business that is known for its silos lack of knowledge sharing (where the belief is that your value is reliant on having information others don't have), I planned to develop this in an iterative way. I established the foundations of the framework and then made adaptations that were appropriate for the business based on the inputs I gathered every time I shared the approach with a stakeholder. This not only ensured my output was well informed with meaningful and relevant business insights but also created a sense of shared ownership; it is far easier to get behind a solution if you are part of the team that shapes it. In one of these stakeholder sessions, the individual not only supported my vision and approach, but he told me directly that he had some of these ideas himself some time ago; now he's going to make sure he circulates them so that he can be sure that "he gets the credit" for them. My colleague and I did our best to suppress our shock: We knew these attitudes existed, but we never expected them to be voiced so directly.

The preceding demonstrates, in my view, the biggest challenge and the most fun part of organizational culture change. Referring to Schein's three levels of culture, most organizations will address the first two, more superficial layers. Artifacts (as seen in team structures like Agile pods), or espoused beliefs and values (such as the establishment of a philosophy of collaboration), are relatively easy to set up. It is the underlying assumptions—the unconscious thoughts, beliefs, feelings, and perceptions that people hold that drive their actions and behaviors—that need to be fundamentally addressed for meaningful, long-term, and penetrative change to occur. Change on this level requires much more than the odd workshop; it requires—again, in my view—the innovation leadership to wear the hat of a coach or a kind of professional therapist as well. This is because, after all, addressing unconscious assumptions requires a psychologically safe place from which to start, and it's a journey that will be slow and beyond most comfort zones (Edmonson, 1999; Schein, 2004).

Conflict

Inevitably, working with others, with limited resources available, creates opportunities for conflict and disagreement. Generally, all those interviewed experienced little conflict among their teams. Such issues when related to what direction to move a creative idea forward are managed by Felix through an evaluation process. Questions he asks himself include: Is this a real issue that affects the quality of the project, or is this someone simply being difficult? How passionate is this person on their point of view? How much can their passion be trusted? How much can their experience be trusted? Finally, Will the idea get bought? He says, "The greatest ideas don't always get bought." He therefore views his team as engineers rather than artists. Eventually, he makes the final decision, and has little tolerance for team members that create friction when it is not for the project's greater good (a fairly standard approach for leaders with narcissistic tendencies). Dana often confronts disagreements among her leadership team with regard to prioritizing budgets for retail projects or innovation projects in her organization on a less formalized, case-by-case basis by balancing long-term versus short-terms business goals.

At the team level, Dana has a select group of people she has worked with before and has hired them specifically because of her full understanding of their skill set as well as her familiarity of how best to manage them—thereby minimizing conflicts. Similarly, Felix stated that he builds teams and very rarely inherits them. So as to avoid becoming a poor manager of 30 or 40 reports, he finds five or six people he considers good lieutenants that he understands and who understand him; this allows him to manage them better even if at times his management style is a five-minute conversation in a corridor.

The approach of Eric and Felix, however, seems intentionally designed to avoid conflict: Where possible, individuals are hired who are already indoctrinated in the ways of working of the leader (it would be interesting to understand how they work with teams that have been inherited, and how this dynamic changes).

There is something to be said, however, for encouraging dissent among teams to bring conflict to the surface and empower teams to resolve them together. Conflict cannot always be avoided; what is truly telling about a culture is the way that it manages it when it presents itself. Teams that feel comfortable directly addressing conflict rather than reverting to passive aggression, or suppressing ideas and feelings, are teams that have trust, mutual respect and shared purpose at their core. This is what enables individuals to operate out of their comfort zone to ultimately deliver impactful innovation.

Alex works with his teams by implementing an agile and collaborative approach to connect disciplines; this enables them to come together to find compromises autonomously. Chris also recognizes that conflict can be healthy; creating an environment where disagreement and challenges are welcome reduces groupthink, makes everyone on the team feel their inputs are valuable and valued, and creates environments in which potential issues and risks are raised early on and avoided or mitigated as appropriate—thereby limiting the risk and damage incurred by the innovation leader, the team, and the business as a whole. Organizations like the Silicon Valley household names we all know have this formalized in their process and attribute it to their success. How leaders choose to create this environment is dependent on their styles and the appropriateness of their wider organizational framework. The important thing, however, is that whatever the mechanism used for creating this environment, a space for welcoming constructive conflict should be established (Scott, 2017).

* * *

In light of the role that collaboration plays in digital innovation and the importance of ingraining this philosophy in teams, it would seem reasonable to create a situation in which digital innovation leaders can demonstrate this approach and lead by example. While this already takes place in some way by engaging in open conversations with teams so that leaders and followers alike feel as if they can speak openly about ideas, this has its limitations. Eric acknowledges that team members at times may be hesitant about speaking openly with him, for example.

The establishment of couple leadership in this space would serve as an example to teams, the business, and even the wider industry that the organization takes collaboration seriously and it starts at the top. It has the potential to drive significant culture change throughout the business and, with time, to other businesses. I will explore this model further in the next chapter.

3   The Couple Leadership Model

Distributed Leadership

The argument for distributed leadership is not a new one: Australian C.A. Gibb first proposed the consideration of an alternative view of leadership beyond that of the solo leader. Since Gibb, others have followed suit (Gronn, 2002). In research conducted by Mehra et al. (2006), it was demonstrated that teams perform better under distributed leadership, and given that research by Hirak et al. (2012) illustrated that the removal of the fear of failure—which is so prevalent in the inherently risky role of innovation leadership—correlates with positive performance, there is an argument to be made that the distribution, or sharing, of risk through distributed leadership would consequently lead to greater success. Grint's (2005) research would seem to also take this view; Grint and others would like to see leadership discussed not in terms of an individual hero-like or deity-type figure but a characteristic possessed by others on a team (Uhl-Bien et al., 2007).

In recent years, it has been the research of Gronn (2002) to most strongly argue the case for distributed leadership, arguing that the conventional approach of solo leadership may not be appropriate in newer working styles and practices, and the fact that leadership is associated with solo leaders is thinking that is fundamentally flawed. He identifies that transformational and charismatic leadership focus on the influence of individual leaders, and that these leadership styles tend to laud the image of the heroic leader. His 2002 publication discusses distributed leadership from mainly the concertive type (informal, and based on collaborative practices and relationships). However, the alternative, numerative leadership that Gibb was focused on—quite literally, formal leadership responsibilities distributed to more than one individual—is of most interest to this study.

Before the discussion of distributed leadership, it is worth taking a moment to consider why the tendency of heroic leadership persists. Why must the leader be a romanticized into a hero? Kulas et al. (2013) demonstrate the importance of risk-propensity as a defining characteristic of a heroic leader, and raise the point that risk aversion has been strongly linked to organizational decline, making the case all the more for its place in the innovation sector. But as Samuels (2003) makes the case for the "bricoleur" as the underrated leader, he provides a reminder that great change is not always dramatic or revolutionary in nature. The leader who can take fragments of the past and see how they can be reimagined to create something new have the potential to create significant transformations—especially within innovation, where disruptive innovations are few in comparison with incremental innovations.

The tennis champion Arthur Ashe one stated, True heroism is remarkably sober, very undramatic. There is growing acknowledgment that impactful leadership need not be heroic; that what truly drives change are those smaller, incremental, and seemingly inconsequential decisions exercised by what Badaracco (2002) calls "quiet leaders" who are interested in doing what's right rather than seeking glory. However, implicit leadership theory raises awareness of the tendency of individuals to use their preconceived ideas rooted in their past to interpret the world, including their assumptions of what makes a leader. This suggests that if individuals have developed the implicit belief that a leader is influential, high profile, determined, and in control, they will interpret individuals lacking in these characteristics as poor leaders—and will aim to develop those characteristics for themselves should they wish to accept a leadership position, thereby propagating the idea further. Because these beliefs are implicit, they are difficult to address and change. It seems a significant societal change would be required to drive this change: earliest childhood memories are still shaped by traditional heroic leaders in fairy tales and films, and these references continue well after in classical literature, and further research on the subject would be welcomed (Badaracco, 2002; Schyns and Meindl, 2005).

And so, partly as a step in this direction, the consideration of distributed leadership should be made. The research published by Gronn three years prior is of direct relevance, making a strong case for couple leadership. His case study on Timbertop, an Australian school, documented the roles and dynamics between Darling (founder) and Montgomery (first head) as a leadership couple: a largely ignored alternative model to the solo leader. Their leadership, which spanned a decade (1951–1961), is considered highly successful, thriving even across significant geographic distances. Among the advantages Gronn observed with this approach was that role overlap, which reduced the risk of poor decisions as they "cross-checked" each other; a point of interest particularly in risk-dominated fields (Gronn, 1999, 2002).

Gronn cites four reasons for success of this approach: a "well-rehearsed working relationship" (they learned how to get the best out of each other), a "reciprocal moral unity" (trust—even enough to tolerate questioning each other when necessary), enough space for them to individually carry out their roles (autonomy), and their "temperaments blended" (their personalities were a match). This seems to be the optimal condition for most working relationships, however—leadership roles would be no exception. His colleagues Hodgson et al. (1965, P. 486) would add that couples who demonstrate three additional properties, "specialization, differentiation, and complementarity of role tasks" in their ways of working would also result in an optimal and effective unit. It seems that a truly effective unit cannot exist without both: Hodgson et al. have focused on the skills and experience of the individuals, whereas Gronn has focused on the personal, psychological, and emotional factors that make working relationships work (Gronn, 1999).

Worth noting here is the relationship between Darling and Montgomery was a hierarchical one, which implies a dependence on each other, as one individual is accountable for the work of both. This lends itself to the development of strong emotions that have the potential to fuel or challenge the development of a positive relationship. However, there is also the alternative of the peer-to-peer model of couple leadership in which neither individual is a subordinate to the other, and is an additional alternative model to leadership in appropriate circumstances (Gronn, 1999).

Gronn's (1999) case study considers psychological factors for the success of the working relationship, but ultimately determines they did not apply here: it was merely the duality of an ideas man and an action man that harmoniously worked well. He falls short of being prescriptive of the personalities that would best be joined, but this type of duality is recurring in digital innovation, as will be demonstrated in paragraphs to come.

What is evident is, as Ziegler and Degrosky (2008) put forth, "a new leadership paradigm is emerging." The previous "industrial" model of leadership, which was solo-individual-centric and based on actions taken to or for other people, is shifting and making way for a "post-industrial" model that is more relational and based on distributed power, which manifests itself in a more collective and collaborative manner. Interestingly, this is happening in even more unexpected industries, such as the financial sector, as demonstrated earlier this year with the establishment of co-CEOs at a fund management company (Gronn, 1999; Walker, 2019).

We have observed thus far that digital innovation leadership roles are immensely challenging. The high risks of failure, the uncertain internal and external environments, and the breadth of demands and expectations on the leader are arguably too much for a sole individual to assume. Furthermore, although the often volatile and dynamic role may best suit leaders of a typically narcissistic character, these individuals bring with them their own challenges to mitigate. Whereas it has been demonstrated that various academics support the consideration of other, distributed models of leadership to address these issues, the claim in this study is that it is particularly the couple model of leadership that is the most appropriate for digital inno-vation. We can see the seeds of this leadership model being sown from our interview insights.

Established or Inferred Co-Leadership

Among our interviewees, all but one individual expressed that they have a select individual or individuals within their organization with whom they discuss and evaluate ideas and plans. All except for Chris embraced this and saw value in this approach: He claimed a flat structure and self-reliance was more the reality in his role, with which he was very comfortable—although it is unclear if this has always been the case in this past, if his organization wouldn't allow otherwise, and if he possibly has engaged in a co-leadership dynamic in the past without an awareness of doing so.

Dana regularly turns to one of her co-founders:

> [him] having been on the retail side, having been on the tech side . . . that's important, we have internal debates . . . and then we come together and have internal debates based on the debates, the informa-tion that we've gathered. There's a lot of knowledge transfer.

Felix finds a "lieutenant" who works under him not only frees up his time, but creates the opportunity for greater impact and influence through "good cop, bad cop" tactics and the like. Even more interestingly, Brian sees its value in the making of more balanced decisions which include both creative and practical perspectives: ". . . it does come down to really the kind of Jon-athan Ive [and] Steve Jobs relationship where you have someone who has the insight, and someone who makes the call who says this is how it is. . . ."

The Apple reference is a common one, also made in the past using the Steve Jobs and Tim Cook relationship, but the structure remains the same: One individual provides the creative, ideation, and strategic expertise while the other provides a practical, operational, and feasible viewpoint. These roles cover two of the three roles outlined by Mumford et al., idea generation and idea structuring (the third, idea promotion, is arguably a responsibility of both parties if the argument in favor of it will hold real weight in the busi-ness). It provides both the creative as well as the strategic leadership outlined by Makri and Scandura, and a "Mr. Creativity" and "Mr. Discipline" as a means by which Deschamps discusses responsibility division (Deschamps, 2008; Makri and Scandura, 2010; Mumford et al., 2002). Brian continues:

> I probably have that with our finance director. It's a really interesting balance . . . between the more visionary, more arty side of innovation in

terms of that perception, and the Tim Cook, kind of hard numbers, will this work and how will it work. . . . I do think actually in that decision-making dynamic you do need a ying and yang between art and science in terms of what are the numbers, what is the commercial opportunity, and then what is the vision and what could that look like. So I think actually, that kind of ying and yang is essential to making good innovation decisions.

Eric relies on his business partner to undergo this same process, and his contribution provides many insights into couple leadership:

It's good to have somebody there that questions things . . . to be honest with us. There's always going to be the sense that somebody (else) might think, "I wouldn't dare say that" for fear or whatever, reprisals, etc. but when you have a partner in that sense there's no concern because you're equals. And we have blazing rows all the time like a married couple, but it's healthy, well from my perspective it is because no one's ever sitting, stewing on something. . . . Because I know full well that if they don't like that idea then I'll know and vice versa.

This particular contribution demonstrates these two leaders do not always agree and are comfortable questioning each other: a key ingredient for the success of couple leadership as put forth by Gronn (2002). Interestingly, he also indirectly makes a case for the peer-to-peer model of couple leadership; he indicates the value that comes from more straightforward talk and open honesty which is more easily derived from a "partner" relationship in which one is not a subordinate to the other and there is no negative repercussion on the individual for a difference of opinion. He continues:

So I think having that sort of relationship is brilliant because it breeds honesty and it forces you to think before you act, because you know it's going to be checked, it's going to be rationalized, so it makes for a better business I think. It's good to have a partnership.

This further demonstrates explicitly how couple leadership leads to more sensible decisions ("it's going to be checked, it's going to be rationalized"). Eric effectively expresses here that couple leadership directly leads to a reduction in risk, and consequently, failure in digital innovation. Furthermore, ". . . you get emotional support as well . . . I like collaborative working . . . it's nice to have somebody to share in the successes and also to scratch heads with when you've got a problem and you need to solve it."

This directly supports the idea that this approach ties in with collaborative working. In a sector that is so dependent on collaboration within a team, across multiple teams, or even across businesses, it would be shortsighted not to consider the benefits that would arise from collaboration at the leadership level. And further to this, there is an argument that leaders should lead by example: A couple leadership model is a strong example for the entire organization that it lives the collaboration culture it wants to embed down the line: ". . . a wall to bounce ideas off. It's good to always have that, and stops people from becoming megalomaniacs."

Finally, Eric underlines its effectiveness of couple leadership in reducing destructive narcissistic tendencies, or "megalomaniacs." There is a "check" in place to curb such behavior and keep leaders more grounded in this leadership model.

The data collected and highlighted previously clearly demonstrates the value of couple leadership. With the outlined benefits and the trend toward couple leadership, the formal widespread acceptance of this leadership model in a formal organizational structure would seem a logical step forward.

Auto-Ethnographical Case Study

For nearly a year, I had the opportunity to work with Felix in a couple leadership model. We had worked together before, but not in the hierarchical structure he expected in this instance. Although it was not obvious at first, it became apparent that the responsibilities were divided in such a way that that he owned the responsibilities of the creative role whereas I owned those of the operational role.

He enjoyed the role of the charismatic leader and strong personality who built the client relationships and made impactful presentations. My role was, as he described it on my first day, to "make him look good." In practice, this meant that I kept development teams working to schedule and budget, and kept the both of us on time, and prepared us both for meetings with clients and suppliers.

Our partnership was a great success; the project we engaged with the client on was extended from a three-month engagement to one that would have gone well into a year and a half had we not accepted other professional opportunities. Our project work served as an example in our client's organization as well as our own, and we quickly established ourselves as the duo who made great things happen—and in record time, at that. Before our arrival, digital projects typically underwent a review-reject-revise-review cycle between project sponsor and review board that took 22 months on average to complete; in our case, the first phase of our project was approved in a mere week's time, no further changes necessary.

We can apply Gronn's framework (2002) to outline why this relationship worked so well:

- We had a well-rehearsed working relationship.
- We had worked together previously and understood how to get the best out of each other.
- We shared mutual trust as well as respect, so when one questioned the other it was evaluated and taken seriously.
- We had autonomy in that while we worked very closely as a working unit, we left each other to get the job done in the knowledge it would be done well.
- Our personalities were complementary and matched very well: This person was not only a colleague but also a respected peer and friend with whom I found collaboration to be rewarding and enjoyable.

To add the perspectives of Hodgson et al. (1965) as well, our roles also were

- Specialized (we both had a high level of expertise that our roles called on)
- Differentiated (divided as described previously through largely creative versus operational objectives)
- Complementary, as we relied on each other to produce optimal work

This leadership approach was not always free of challenges, but in the times they arose it was because one of Gronn's (2002) four conditions was at risk. The relationship became strained on two occasions in which external factors temporarily created cause for doubt and lack of trust—and the relationship was only truly effective again once this was overcome.

The first was one in which I advised him on a manner regarding a creative approach: I recommended one option but he insisted on another, which I felt was wrong for us and wrong for the client. Because the dynamic was a hierarchical one rather than peer-to-peer, there was little I could do. Although the creative requirements fell under his role rather than mine, I found it challenging to accept. In hindsight, if there had been a more clearly defined working model established from the first day, some of the friction might have been reduced, but only to a degree: we both had creative experience in our background and I felt my reasoning was sound and justified. Had we been operating in a peer-to-peer model, I expect that in light of his narcissistic tendencies, we might have still accepted his approach in order to move the project along. In these cases, one must choose one's battles to prioritize winning the war. The self-aware leader should be able to judge appropriately the moments in which the ego must be set aside for the greater good.

The second occasion was at a moment in which I had built a relationship with the client to such a strong state that she wanted my opinion to be the final sign-off and approval point over his own. At this stage of the program of work, the sign-offs on behalf of the client were in relation to creative work, which fell under Felix's remit. It is easy to see how he would have felt threatened as my relationship with the client grew, and I was awarded decision powers in an area he felt was his own. This moment put the trust between us into question and possibly aggravated his more narcissistic tendencies. Ultimately, he managed the situation in such a way as to keep this relationship between the client and me from developing further, and his intentions were facilitated by her impending departure on maternity leave.

In spite of these challenges, those who observed our working model often acknowledged it was quite clearly an effective and productive dynamic, and created the conditions for optimal growth and success. We both benefitted from bouncing ideas off of each other, validating each other's thinking and having an outlet in which to vent frustrations. The project also benefitted because our different personalities matched with different types of stakeholders, and we were able to leverage our respective relationships to drive change and progress. Finally, in a constantly changing landscape in which the clients and stakeholders were regularly changing as a consequence of an ongoing merger and acquisition, it was invaluable to have a constant in the project that could be trusted and relied upon.

This couple leadership model was one of the most rewarding dynamics I have worked in, and one of the most successful projects for which either of us have been responsible: I would welcome the opportunity to operate in such a leadership model again in the future.

Practical Application of the Model

Consider the following points as your guidance in putting the model into practice.

For Organizations Hiring Into a Couple Leadership Model

It's important to remember that this model isn't a panacea: No two people, however capable or brilliant they might be, can overcome issues like deep-rooted unhealthy organizational cultures alone and consistently deliver great innovative work. But, given sufficient autonomy and influence, they can create positive environments in which innovation thrives.

Table 3.1 Hard and Soft Factors in the Hiring Process

Hard factors	Soft factors
Specialization	A well-rehearsed working relationship
Differentiation	Reciprocal moral unity
Complementarity of role tasks	Autonomy
	Temperaments that blend

If you are formally establishing the leadership model in your organizational structure, it may take some adjustment for the team. With the solo leader model so deeply ingrained in the societal psyche, it is likely that team members will be looking to understand which of the two is the dominant character, or the "real leader." For this reason, I would strongly advise that your first organization's first experience with couple leadership be on a peer-to-peer basis.

A very rudimentary breakdown of hard and soft qualities you should be looking for in your hiring process is shown in Table 3.1.

It is likely that you are already familiar with hiring for specialization; a skills-based search is usually a default for most organizations. I also imagine you will find it easier to hire a specialist that can cover some—instead of all—of the disciplines you need to support. The challenge will be to find an individual that will cover the gaps that the first of two hires will have for this leadership function. In other words, the second hire ensures you have accounted for the differentiated and complementary skills that complete the left column in Table 3.1. For example, let's assume you have found a candidate with innovation leadership experience—perhaps at a challenger bank, where he or she had predominantly operational and financial accountability. Your second leader might well come from a creative or perhaps a strategy background.

When hiring for the roles, you may want to consider hiring a leader that has his or her own co-leader with whom there is already a trusted and proven working relationship. It may sound like a needle in a haystack to find such a dynamic, but most professionals who have reached this stage of their career will have, by this point, built a trusted network of people they would gladly work with again. If instead you are looking to hire one individual to take on a co-leadership structure with someone new, then your hired individual should take on a proactive role in selecting their co-leader to account for those soft qualities and determine if there is natural working chemistry. If you are hiring someone to work with a long-time staff member, then this is just as important.

Because, you see, hiring for those soft qualities will be the greatest challenge in the process. Yes, you may be able to determine if there is a match of temperaments and personalities at the interview stage—and for this assessment, I might suggest finding a more natural setting than your office space for these two to see how well they get on with each other (a coffee shop or restaurant, or perhaps a shared activity of some kind). But giving each other autonomy, and being tolerant or even welcoming to challenges from the other person, both rely an essential, valuable and rare commodity: trust. The final characteristic—that of a well-rehearsed working relationship—is something that is built over time if the two individuals haven't worked together previously, but it is enabled by the other three and developed on the basis of trust. Sacrificing one of these four factors will not bring the results you are looking for.

Now, it is out of the scope of this volume to explore trust building with at least the minimum degree of depth required to respectfully address the topic. But if two individuals like each other's company and show natural chemistry (temperament), if they respect each other (specialization) and rely on each other (differentiation, complimentary skills) to achieve the same, mutually desired objective, then it is perfectly reasonable that they have the right foundation in place to let each other get on with their work (autonomy) and would welcome the other person sense-checking their thinking in the face of big or risky decisions. If at any point trust is lost (one of the two feels at risk of being thrown under the metaphorical bus, their autonomy is removed through micro-management or undermining, etc.) then the effectiveness of this dynamic will be impacted.

Although not a formal part of the model, I would reiterate that in the evaluation of temperaments, effort is made to assess for a high degree of emotional intelligence. It isn't enough that your leaders get along well; they need to have the emotional agility to manage challenges, fears, and the values of others—not only between themselves but also among their teams and the wider organizations.

A final word on structural dynamic of these two individuals: Be it a peer-to-peer or a hierarchical model, it's imperative that the responsibilities over the roles are clearly defined and adhered to without undermining the other individual, and it is important not to undermine the choices and decisions taken by the co-leader. If not, the understanding within the organization will be that there is only one leader and a delegate—and you will have doubled your payroll for this leadership function without reaping the rewards you are seeking.

For Digital Innovation Leaders Adopting the Model

Hopefully you have a sufficient degree of self-awareness to understand your own strengths and weaknesses so that you understand what kind of profile would be complementary to you. For example, if you are a visionary leader with no patience for the numbers or the details of the planning, there is no point in taking on the full demands of the role; your partner should compensate for with strengths such as attention to detail and concern for how your visions will actually manifest.

It is likely that in this stage of your career, you have come across individuals who are a balance to you and with whom working together is a proven relationship. These are colleagues that form part of your network, with whom you have already established ways of working that are optimal and lead to great work. For the right organization, it may be possible to you to arrive as a pair, but more likely the first of you will land in the role and bring on the other individual.

In light of the framework discussed here, take care in considering the relationship and understanding if those key factors we've addressed are present. As we have seen from the case study, where that is not the case, the impact will eventually be felt by the both of you and the wider organization—and quite likely, your client.

Performance Assessment

I am not, nor have I ever been, a professional human resources lead. As such, I have no intention of defining a fully detailed performance evaluation strategy for digital innovation leaders in couple leadership capacities. However, it would be remiss of me not to include some considerations and possible approaches that I believe should be part of your process (aside from the elements from the framework that were used to hire into the roles initially):

- *Direct feedback from your co-leaders*: They should be seen as a unit and might possibly warrant an assessment together. If the right cultural foundations are set, the airing of strengths and weaknesses on performance should (1) feel safe to participate in and (2) not reveal anything that the two don't already know about each other. I would be concerned if the latter is not the case; it might be a symptom of a difficulty within their dynamic.
- *Feedback collected from the team*: the most valuable feedback is that which is related to culture, such as:
  - How comfortable does the team feel proposing new ideas, or challenging others?
  - How comfortable are they with risk-taking? Are they willing to take sensible chances for innovation because they feel their careers will not be penalized for it?
  - How much satisfaction do they feel with their roles?

- Is the team attrition rate higher or lower than average?
- How supportive do they find their innovation leaders are with regards to their career development, idea generation, and more?
- How much trust do they have in their innovation leaders—to do the right thing, make sensible decisions, to look after the team?

- *Collaboration*: The most meaningful way to assess this is not to determine whether or not teams have been structured for this, or supporting tooling has been set up; rather, it is through engagement.

  - How frequently are team members speaking up with new ideas or challenges?
  - Is "out-of-the-box" thinking cultivated?
  - How frequently are new ideas for innovation—from within the team or the wider organization—being generated?
  - What is the attendance and participation like in meetings, brainstorming sessions, and more?
  - How willing are team members pitching in to support others to work together for the greater goal?

- *Perception*: How the wider business perceives these leaders and their dynamic should be taken with a pinch of salt; new ideas and challenges are rarely welcomed with enthusiasm. But, there is value in assessing this if the intention is to not only determine the perception, but the underlying reasons for that perception, to determine if their evidence-based opinions have validity. Other criteria to consider would be the enthusiasm and desire of other teams to join your co-leaders in their department and, once the leadership model is established, any responses from outside the organization and among the industry. If you are among the first to adopt this model, you may consider whether competitors are adopting this approach as well and consider this as a sign of success.

- *Inspired and creative ideas and strategies*: assessing leaders for ideas is thorny; the value of an idea is often not realized until sometime after its development, and idea generation should not come from one person alone. However, it is possible to assess the pipeline of ideas:

  - Are there ideas regularly being proposed that are viable (support the business strategy), feasible (can be achieved with the resources the business has or can acquire), and desirable (is there a demand for it)?
  - Is there a variety of channels from which ideas can be collected—both from within the business as well as from the wider marketplace?
  - Are there occasionally ideas that are "pioneer" ideas, or are they predominantly building on already existing products and

approaches? (There is no negative answer here; the important thing is that the business strategy supports this. If being a strong follower is more important than breaking into a new area, then incremental improvements are perfectly acceptable.)

- *Long-term ROI*: Hopefully, it is understood that most investments in digital innovation or transformation do not result in an immediate return on investment (ROI); that is part of their inherent risk. However, unless one is working as a volunteer or a non-profit business, a financial performance indicator will inevitably be a key metric for most organizations. The caveat that I would apply in the assessment of this metric is that it is evaluated with the distance of time. I appreciate this is challenging in light of the average turnover rates of digital professionals; one way to mitigate a big up-front investment is to develop and release in iterations, as so many projects and programs in the digital space typically do. However, bear in mind that incremental releases may well drive incremental returns.

A possible approach to consider is the means by which bonuses on performance are allocated. I am proud to presently work for an organization where only a minority percentage of annual bonus is based on personal performance; the remaining percentage is based on factors such as the degree to which you support the ideas of your peers to bring them to fruition, and the degree to which you support the more junior members of the team to create opportunities for them to grow and develop their full potential. It is when organizations truly put their money where their mouth is that the deepest levels of cultural impact can be attained.

Conclusion

In the preceding pages we've reviewed literature related to innovation and leadership, including models and frameworks, and themes such as risk, failure, narcissism, and heroism. We've explored new qualitative research aimed to provide new insight on the innovation leadership role: its challenges, difficulties, demands, and requirements. Finally, I have proposed a new leadership model—couple leadership—as the appropriate default model for this unique leadership requirement, which is becoming ever more prevalent, demonstrated a working case study, and provided recommendations for implementation.

Argument Summary

This book puts forth the argument that the couple leadership model is optimal for the leadership responsibilities of digital innovation; it mitigates many challenges while providing added benefits—to digital leaders, their internal teams, the wider organization, and, indirectly, possibly the industry as well.

A wider distribution of pressure and responsibility over innovation successes and risk provides ultimately a fairer performance appraisal in which the success or failure of a project fundamentally filled with uncertainty does not rest on the shoulders of one individual. The timeless cliché that "two heads are better than one" holds true: a second perspective provides greater clarity, encourages diversity of thought, reduces risk, and leads to better decisions as a principle. This is particularly appropriate for businesses in the scope of this study for which an innovation governance committee is inappropriate.

Such collaborative leadership also provides an opportunity for leadership through example: digital innovation by its innately collaborative nature lends itself to the couple leadership model, which offers the opportunity to represent and demonstrate collaborative working. And, as such a model removes the focus on the solo leader, the typical risks and challenges associated with leaders of the narcissistic or hero persona are mitigated through the provision of a sidekick, or partner, to reduce the impact of negative tendencies. Of particular importance, because this structure challenges the deepest cultural level of assumptions and beliefs regarding what leadership is, it creates a catalyst for meaningful organizational culture change needed for digital innovation that does not occur with mere workshops or team restructures.

Furthermore, independent research indicates there is already a tendency to move in this direction in a variety of organizations, as we have seen the duality of creative and organizational, ideas and action, reoccurring. The couple leadership model would merely formalize and capitalize on a means of leadership that has already started taking shape quite naturally (Walker, 2019).

Recommended Further Research

It should be said that the research conducted has been by no means exhaustive on this topic, and more extensive research into other related areas— many also highlighted by other researchers in this space—would prove valuable.

Some particular areas of interest include the enactment and study of innovation successes under the couple leadership model; the collaboration and team atmosphere that results under couple leadership; more extensive research into the differences between leadership couples on equal footing versus those comprised of super- and sub-ordinates; the challenge of transitioning into a couple leadership model, from both a practical and psychological perspective; the importance of trust and betrayal aversion in the face of risk as a key factor; and a more suitable means by which to re-conceptualize and analyze leadership, which thus far appears to be best suited to the heroic, or, at least, the solo leader. Finally, valuable contributions would be made in the further research on how implicit theories can be addressed and changed from a wider societal perspective, and the implications a mixed gender couple leadership combination could have on the advancement of gender equality.

Acknowledgements

I began our journey through these pages with one of my favorite Andrew Carnegie quotes: "No man will make a great leader who wants to do it all himself, or to get all the credit for doing it." It is in this spirit that I spare a moment to acknowledge those who have made this body of work possible with their support, feedback, and encouragement—initially at the dissertation phase, and then in its evolution into this volume.

I would first like to thank two individuals from Warwick Business School. My profound gratitude goes to Dr. Jose Bento da Silva for his patient supervision, guidance, and continued encouragement during the dissertation phase, and his support once again in the process of developing this present volume. I would also be remiss not to acknowledge Dr. Hari Tsoukas, whose inspirational module "Leadership and the Art of Judgement" ignited my passion and pursuit of leadership studies.

I would also like to extend my gratitude to all those who sacrificed their time to take part in the interviews that informed my dissertation. Their contributions provided rich insight into the role of today's leaders in digital innovation, and have been invaluable in drawing the conclusions presented in these pages.

My heartfelt appreciation goes to my friends for the continued support throughout the period of study and research. Their friendship and understanding—be it in social celebrations I have sacrificed for academic pursuits or the care they've offered to me in challenging moments—have made all the difference. Thanks to Mariam and Carla, who nourished my soul over dinners and tea so that I could remain focused during the research phase; Tanya and Craig, who offered the same support over brunches and coffees in the developments of both the dissertation and the volume you have just read; Chris and Nick, who were pillars of strength in the last several challenging months of the first phase of this project; and Maryah, who not only continued to remind me of the faith she had in me during the more difficult stages of completing this exciting project, but provided her editing expertise to much of this content—and in record time at that. Thanks also to FD, who has challenged and inspired me personally and professionally for much of my journey.

My final note of gratitude is dedicated to my parents. For my mother Isabella, who taught me that access to knowledge and an education—particularly for my gender—is a privileged opportunity that should never be taken for granted; and for my father Matteo, who instilled in me from a young age the discipline and resilience required to complete such an endeavor.

Bibliography

151 Pt. 10. Congressional Record 13510. (20–27 June 2005). Available from: https://library.uvm.edu/guides/citation/CitingGovernmentInfo.pdf (Accessed 6 Feb 2016).

Attride-Stirling, Jennifer. (2011). Thematic Networks: An Analytic Tool for Qualitative Research. *Qualitative Research*, 1 (3): 385–405.

Badaracco, Joseph L., Jr. (2002). *Leading Quietly: An Unorthodox Guide to Doing the Right Thing*. Boston: Harvard Business Review Press.

Campbell, A., Whitehead, J. & Finkelstein, S. (Feb 2009). Why Good Leaders Make Bad Decisions. *Harvard Business Review*: 60–66.

Casserly, Meghan. (2002). 10 Jobs That Didn't Exist 10 Years Ago [Online]. *Forbes*. Available from: www.forbes.com/sites/meghancasserly/2012/05/11/10-jobs-that-didnt-exist-10-years-ago/2/#7b37fe6849b5 (Accessed 19 Feb 2016).

CIPD. Health and Well-Being at Work: Survey Report. (Apr 2019). Available from: www.cipd.co.uk/Images/health-and-well-being-at-work-2019.v1_tcm18-55881.pdf (Accessed 5 Aug 2019).

CNBC. (2016). 10 Jobs That Weren't Around in 1989 [Online]. *CNBC*. Available from: www.cnbc.com/2014/04/29/10-jobs-that-werent-around-in-1989.html?slide=1 (Accessed 19 Feb 2016).

Compton-Hall, Jim. (2014). 6 Creative Jobs That Didn't Exist 10 Years Ago [Online]. *FutureRising*. Available from: www.futurerising.com/6-creative-jobs-that-didnt-exist-10-years-ago (Accessed 19 Feb 2016).

Conforth, Chris & Brown, William A. (2014). *Nonprofit Governance: Innovative Perspectives and Approaches*. New York: Routledge.

Coutu, Diane L. (Jan 2004). Putting Leaders on the Couch: A Conversation with Manfred F.R. Kets de Vries. *Harvard Business Review*: 64–71.

Deschamps, J. (2008). *Innovation Leaders*. San Francisco: Wiley.

Deschamps, J. & Nelson, B. (2014). *Innovation Governance: How Top Management Organises and Mobilizes for Innovation*. San Francisco: Wiley.

Edmonson, Amy. (1999). Psychological Safety and Learning Behavior in Work Teams. *Administrative Science Quarterly*, 44 (2), ABI/INFORM Global: 350.

Ellis, Carolyn. (2004). *The Ethnographic I: A Methodological Novel about Autoethnography*. Walnut Creek: AltaMira Press.

Ellis, Carolyn, Adams, T. E. & Bochner, A. (2011). Autoethnography: An Overview. *Historical Social Research/Historische Sozialforschung*, 36 (4 (138)): 273–290. Available from: www.jstor.org/stable/23032294 (Accessed 3 Aug 2015).

Epstein, David. (2019). *Range: Why Generalists Triumph in a Specialized World*. New York: Riverhead Books.

Finley, Klint. (2013). New Study Exposes Gender Bias in Tech Job Listings [Online]. *Wired*. Available from: www.wired.com/2013/03/hiring-women/ (Accessed 19 Feb 2016).

Flick, Uwe. (2009). *An Introduction to Qualitative Research: 4th Edition*. London: Sage Publications.

Giessner, S.R., Van Knippenberg, D. & Sleebos, E. (2009). License to Fail? How Leader Group Prototypicality Moderates the Effects of Leader Performance on Perceptions of Leadership Effectiveness. *The Leadership Quarterly*, 20 (3): 434–451.

Gilpin, Lyndsey. (2014). The State of Women in Technology: 15 Data Points You Should Know [Online]. *TechRepublic*. Available from: www.techrepublic.com/article/the-state-of-women-in-technology-15-data-points-you-should-know/ (Accessed 9 Jan 2016).

Goleman, Daniel. (2004). What Makes a Leader? *Harvard Business Review*, 82 (1): 82–91.

Grint, K. (2005). *Leadership: Limits and Possibilities*. Basingstoke: Palgrave MacMillan.

Gronn, P. (1999). Substituting for Leadership: The Neglected Role of the Leadership Couple. *The Leadership Quarterly*, 10 (1): 41–62.

Gronn, P. (2002). Distributed Leadership as a Unit of Analysis. *The Leadership Quarterly*, 13 (4): 423–451.

Hall, A.T., Blass, F.R., Ferris, G.R. & Massengale, Randy. (2004). Leader Reputation and Accountability in Organisations: Implications for Dysfunctional Leader Behavior. *The Leadership Quarterly*, 15: 515–536.

Hanna, Paul. (Apr 2012). Using Internet Technologies (Such as Skype) as a Research Medium: A Research Note. *Qualitative Research*, 12: 239–242.

Hirak, R., Peng, A.C., Carmeli, A. & Schaubroeck, J.M. (2012). Linking Leader Inclusiveness to Work Unit Performance: The Importance of Psychological Safety and Learning From Failures. *The Leadership Quarterly*, 23 (1): 107–117.

Hodgson, R.C., Levinson, D.J. & Zaleznik, A. (1965). *The Executive Role Constellation: An Analysis of Personality and Role Relations in Management*. Boston: Harvard University Press.

Innovaro. (2008). *Innovation Leaders*. Oxford: Infinite Ideas Ltd.

Interview A. (2015). *Leadership and Digital Innovation on 1 September*. London.

Interview B. (2015). *Leadership and Digital Innovation on 10 September*. London.

Interview C. (2015). *Leadership and Digital Innovation on 11 September*. London.

Interview D. (2015). *Leadership and Digital Innovation on 3 September*. London.

Interview E. (2015). *Leadership and Digital Innovation on 10 September*. London.

Interview F. (2015). *Leadership and Digital Innovation on 27 August*. London.

Kahan, Seth. (2013). *Getting Innovation Right: How Leaders Leverage Inflection Points to Drive Success*. San Francisco: Wiley.

Kahneman, Daniel. (2012). *Thinking, Fast and Slow*. London: Penguin Books.

Kaplan, Soren. (2012). Fear of Failure Is the Big Problem, Not Failure Itself [Online]. *Innovation Excellence*. Available from: www.innovationexcellence.com/blog/2012/08/07/fear-of-failure-is-the-big-problem-not-failure-itself/?Itemid=92 (Accessed 9 Jan 2016).

King, Nigel & Horrocks, Christine. (2010). *Interviews in Qualitative Research*. London: Sage Publications.

Kollee, J.A.J.M., Giessner, S.R. & Van Knippenberg, D. (2013). Leader Evaluations after Performance Feedback: The Role of the Follower Mood. *The Leadership Quarterly*, 24 (1): 203–214.

Kotler, P., Armstrong, G., Wong, V. & Saunders, J. (2008). *Principles of Marketing*. Harlow: Pearson.

Kruse, Kevin. (2012). 100 Best Quotes on Leadership [Online]. *Forbes*. Available from: www.forbes.com/sites/kevinkruse/2012/10/16/quotes-on-leadership/#67119dfc7106 (Accessed 16 Feb 2016).

Kulas, J.T., Komai, M. & Grossman, P.J. (2013). Leadership, Information and Risk Attitude: A Game Theoretic Approach. *The Leadership Quarterly*, 24: 349–362.

Maccoby, Michael. (2004). Narcissistic Leaders: The Incredible Pros, the Inevitable Cons. *Harvard Business Review*, January: 92–101.

Makri, M. & Scandura, T.A. (2010). Exploring the Effects of Creative CEO Leadership on Innovation in High-Technology Firms. *The Leadership Quarterly*, 21: 75–88.

Maniscalco, Caterina. (2016). *Professional Experiences and Career Reflections*. Unpublished.

Mehra, A., Smith, B.R., Dixon, A.L. & Robertson, B. (2006). Distributed Leadership In Teams: The Network of Leadership Perceptions and Team Performance. *The Leadership Quarterly*, 17 (3): 232–245.

Miller, T., Birch, M., Mauthner, M. & Jessop, J. (2012). *Ethics in Qualitative Research*. London: Sage Publications.

Mumford, M.D. & Connelly, M.S. (1991). Leaders as Creators: Leader Performance and Problem Solving in Ill-Defined Domains. *The Leadership Quarterly*, 2 (4): 289–315.

Mumford, M.D. & Licuanan, B. (2004). Leading for Innovation: Conclusions, Issues and Directions. *The Leadership Quarterly*, 15 (1): 163–171.

Mumford, M.D., Scott, G.M., Gaddis, S.B. & Strange, J.M. (2002). Leading Creative People: Orchestrating Expertise and Relationships. *The Leadership Quarterly*, 13: 705–750.

Nevicka, B., De Hoogh, A.H.B., Van Vianen, A.E.M., Beersma, B. & McIlwain, D. (2011). All I Need is a Stage to Shine: Narcissists' Leader Emergence and Performance. *The Leadership Quarterly*, 22 (5): 910–925.

Offermann, L.R., Kennedy, J.K. & Wirtz, P.W. (1994). Implicit Leadership Theories: Content, Structure, and Generalizability. *The Leadership Quarterly*, 5 (1): 43–58.

Opdenakker, Raymond. (2006). Advantages and Disadvantages of Four Interview Techniques in Qualitative Research [Online]. *Forum Qualitative Sozialforschung/Forum: Qualitative Social Research*, 7 (4). Available from: www.qualitative-research.net/index.php/fqs/article/view/175/391 (Accessed 25 Nov 2015).

Pink, Daniel H. (2011). *Drive*. Edinburgh: Cannongate Books.

Robson, C. (1993). *Real World Research*. Oxford: Blackwell.

Samuels, Richard J. (2003). When Leadership Failed. *The American Sociologist*, 34 (1): 33–44.

Schein, Edgard H. (2004). *Organizational Culture and Leadership: 3rd Edition*. San Francisco: Jossey-Bass.

Schoellkopf, Karen. (2014). Hire More Women in Tech [Online]. Available from: www.hiremorewomenintech.com/ (Accessed 19 Feb 2016).

Schyns, B. & Meindl, J.R. (2005). *Implicit Leadership Theories: Essays and Explorations*. Charlotte: Information Age Publishing.

Scott, Kim. (2017). *Radical Candor*. New York: St. Martin's Press.

Scouller, James. (2011). *The Three Levels of Leadership*. Cirencester: Management Books 2000.

Smart Insights. (2015). The Evolution of Digital Skills [Online]. *Smart Insights*. Available from: www.smartinsights.com/managing-digital-marketing/personal-career-development/digital-skills/ (Accessed 16 Feb 2016).

Stein, Mark. (2013). When Does Narcissistic Leadership become Problematic? *Journal of Management Inquiry*, 22 (3): 282–293.

Sternberg, Robert J. (2003). WICS: A Model of Leadership in Organisations. *Academy of Management Learning and Education*, 2 (4): 386–401.

Sternberg, Robert J. & Vroom, V. (2002). The Person Versus the Situation in Leadership. *The Leadership Quarterly*, 13: 301–323.

Sternberg, Robert J., et al. (2003). A Propulsion Model of Creative Leadership. *The Leadership Quarterly*, 14: 455–476.

Syed, Matthew. (Dec 2015). Ideas Bank. *Wired*: 93.

Uhl-Bien, Mary Marion, Russ & McKelvey, Bill. (2007). Complexity Leadership Theory: Shifting Leadership from the Industrial Age to the Knowledge Era. *The Leadership Quarterly*, 18 (4): 298–318.

Walker, Owen. (27 Jan 2019). Martin Gilbert and Keith Skeoch: Flying the Flag for Co-CEOs [Online]. *Financial Times*. Available from: https://on.ft.com/2DERzVX (Accessed 2 Feb 2019).

Westley, F. & Mintzberg, H. (1989). Visionary Leadership and Strategic Management. *Strategic Management Journal*, 10: 17–32.

Wilson, Josh. (2018). Work-Related Stress and Mental Illness Now Accounts for over Half of Work Absences [Online]. *The Telegraph*. Available from: www.telegraph.co.uk/news/2018/11/01/work-related-stress-mental-illness-now-accounts-half-work-absences/ (Accessed 5 Aug 2019).

Ziegler, J. & DeGrosky, M. (2008). Managing the Meaning of Leadership: Leadership as 'Communicating Intent' in Wildland Firefighting. *Leadership*, 4 (3): 271–297, Scopus®, EBSCO*host* (accessed 6 Feb 2016).

Index

Note: Page numbers in **bold** indicate a table on the corresponding page.

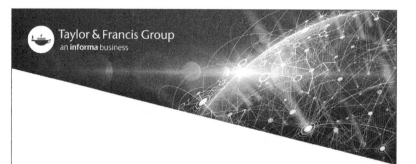

Printed in the United States
by Baker & Taylor Publisher Services

Printed in the United States
by Baker & Taylor Publisher Services